OCR GCSE (9-1)
Computer Science

S. Robson

P.M. Heathcote

Published by
PG Online Limited

The Old Coach House
35 Main Road
Tolpuddle
Dorset
DT2 7EW
United Kingdom

sales@pgonline.co.uk
www.pgonline.co.uk
2016

PG ONLINE

Acknowledgements

We are grateful to the OCR (Oxford Cambridge and RSA Examinations) for permission to use questions from past papers.

The answers in the Teacher's Supplement are the sole responsibility of the authors and have neither been provided nor approved by the examination boards.

We would also like to thank the following for permission to reproduce copyright photographs:

Server Room © Google/Connie Zhou

How Secure is My Password screenshot © RoboForm, Siber Systems, Inc

PayPal screenshot © PayPal Inc

Other photographic images © Shutterstock

Ocado shopping image © Ocado Limited

Cover picture © 'Waresley Wood I' 2013
Acrylic on canvas, 21cm x 23cm
Reproduced with the kind permission of Charlotte Cornish
www.charlottecornish.co.uk

Cover artwork, graphics and typesetting by PG Online Ltd

First edition 2016, reprinted 2016, 2017, 2018

Preface

This is a brand new book from two popular and experienced authors. Aimed at GCSE students, it provides comprehensive yet concise coverage of all the topics covered in the new J276 Computer Science specification, written and presented in a way that is accessible to teenagers. It can be used as a course text and as assessment preparation for students nearing the end of their course.

It is divided into eight sections covering every element of the specification. Sections 5 and 6 of the textbook cover algorithms and programming concepts with a theoretical approach to provide students with experience of writing, tracing and debugging pseudocode solutions without the aid of a computer. These sections would complement practical programming experience.

Each chapter contains exercises and questions, some from past examination papers, and answers to all these are available to teachers only in a free Teachers Supplement which can be ordered from our website **www.pgonline.co.uk**.

Contents

Section 1

Systems architecture, memory and storage

Objectives

- Understand the purpose of the CPU

- Explain the role and operation of the following CPU registers used in Von Neumann architecture: MAR (Memory Address Register), MDR (Memory Data Register), Program Counter, Accumulator

- Describe common CPU components and their function: (ALU Arithmetic Logic Unit), CU (Control Unit), Cache

- Explain the function of the CPU as fetch and execute instructions stored in memory

- Describe how common characteristics of CPUs affect their performance: clock speed, cache size, number of cores

- Explain the purpose and give examples of embedded systems

- Describe the difference between RAM and ROM

- Describe the purpose RAM and ROM in a computer system

- Explain the need for virtual memory

- Describe flash memory

- Discuss the need for secondary storage including optical, magnetic and solid state storage

- Discuss data capacity of storage devices and

- Calculate data capacity requirements

- Select suitable storage devices and storage media for a given application and the advantages and disadvantages of these, using characteristics: capacity, speed, portability, durability, reliability, cost

1.1 – The CPU

Basic computer system model

A computer system is made up of hardware and software. Hardware is any physical component that makes up the computer. Software is any program that runs on the computer.

Computer systems are all around us. They are not just the PCs on the desk but include mobile phones, cash machines, supermarket tills and the engine management systems in a modern-day car.

The diagram below shows the basic model of a computer system.

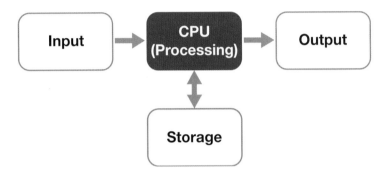

All computer systems must have a **CPU** and at least one **input device** that gets data from the real world. This could be a mouse and keyboard on a conventional PC, a temperature sensor (thermistor) in a commercial greenhouse or the microphone on a mobile phone.

Input devices take real world data and convert it into a form that can be stored on the computer. The input from these devices is processed and the computer system will generate outputs. The **output device** could be, for example, a conventional computer screen, an actuator that opens or closes a greenhouse window, or the speaker that produces sound on a phone.

The fourth component is **storage**. The computer system may need to use stored data to perform the processing and, as a result of processing input, may generate data that is then stored.

Any computer system will have these four basic components.

> Q1 Name three input, output and storage devices.

The purpose of the Central Processing Unit

The **Central Processing Unit** (CPU) of a computer is the hardware that executes programs and manages the rest of the hardware. Think of the CPU as the brain of the computer. Just as your brain contains parts that remember things, parts that think and parts that make the rest of your body operate, the CPU does the same for the computer. The CPU is made up of the main memory, the processor and the cache memory.

Von Neumann architecture

With the very first computers, it was not possible to store programs, and programs were generally input by setting switches. John Von Neumann developed the concept of the stored program computer in the 1940s. The **Von Neumann** architecture used the idea of holding programs in memory and data would then move between the memory unit and the processor.

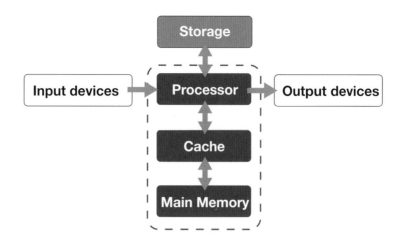

Components of the processor

The processor responds to and processes the instructions that drive the computer. It contains the Control Unit (CU), the Arithmetic Logic Unit (ALU) and registers. The accumulator is a special-purpose, very fast memory location in which results of operations carried out in the ALU are temporarily stored. (N.B. Most processors have several general-purpose registers instead of a single accumulator used as temporary fast storage.)

The program instructions and data move between the main memory and the processor using internal connections called **buses**.

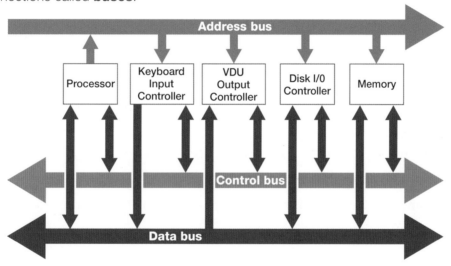

Three types of bus are used:

- Address bus – carries addresses from the processor to memory and input/output devices
- Data bus – sends data between the processor, memory and input/output devices
- Control bus – carries signals to coordinate all the computer activities

> **Q2** Why does data not go to the keyboard controller, or come from the VDU output controller?

Control Unit

The Control Unit coordinates all the activities taking place inside the CPU. Its functions may be summarised as follows:

- It controls the execution of instructions in the correct sequence
- It decodes instructions
- It regulates and controls processor timing using regular pulses from the system clock
- It sends and receives control signals to and from other devices within the computer

The Arithmetic and Logic Unit (ALU)

The ALU carries out the following functions:

- **Logical Operations**: These include AND, OR and NOT
- **Shift Operations**: The bits in a computer word can be shifted left or right by a certain number of places
- **Arithmetic Operations**: These include addition, subtraction, multiplication and division

Special-purpose registers

A register is a special very fast memory location within the CPU used in the execution of instructions.

A CPU has number of special-purpose registers, listed below:

- Memory Address Register (MAR)
- Memory Data Register (MDR)
- Program Counter (PC)
- Current Instruction Register (CIR)
- Accumulator

The **Memory Address Register (MAR)** holds the address (location in memory) of the instruction or piece of data to be fetched or stored.

When the data or program instruction is fetched from memory, it is temporarily held in the **Memory Data Register (MDR)**.

The **Program Counter (PC)** holds the memory address of the next instruction to be processed.

The **Current Instruction Register (CIR)** holds the current instruction to be executed, which has been fetched from memory and is temporarily held in the MDR before being copied to the CIR.

The **Accumulator (ACC)** is one of the general purpose registers in which data and results of many operations are temporarily stored.

For example, the assembly code below fetches a value from main memory, adds 80 to it and stores the result of the addition back into memory.

```
LDA 2560     loads the data at address 2560 into the accumulator (ACC)

ADD #80      adds the value 80 to the present content of the accumulator

STA 2560     stores the content of the accumulator in memory location 2560
```

When you write an instruction in Python or Visual Basic, for example:

```
a = a + 80
```

it is broken down into these three basic instructions and the addition is done in the accumulator.

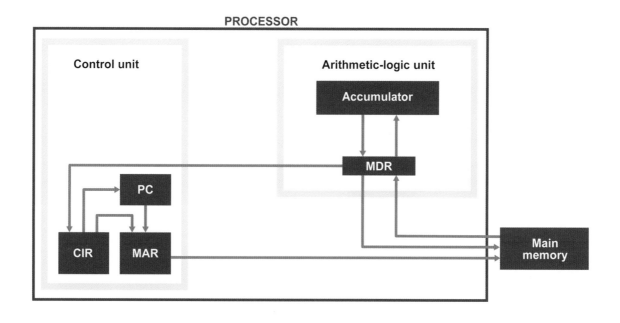

PROCESSOR

Control unit

Arithmetic-logic unit

Accumulator

MDR

PC

CIR   MAR

Main memory

Q3 An instruction is given to fetch the contents of memory location 25 and load it into the accumulator. Describe which registers would be used to allow this fetch operation to take place.

Q4 Suppose address 51 contains the value 40. What value is stored in the accumulator at each stage of the following process? What value would be finally stored address 51?

```
LDA 51   load contents of address 51 into accumulator
SUB #15  subtract the value 15 from accumulator
STA 51   store contents of accumulator in address 51
```

1

1.2 – Function and characteristics of the CPU

Fetch-Decode-Execute cycle

When a program is to be run (executed) on a computer it first has to be loaded into main memory. From here it can be accessed by the processor, which runs each instruction in turn. When the program is loaded, the processor is given the start address of where it is held in main memory. To run the program the processor fetches an instruction, decodes it and then executes it. The processor executes one instruction at a time. This is called the **Fetch-Decode-Execute cycle, or simply the Fetch-Execute cycle.**

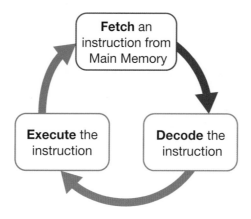

Fetch an instruction from Main Memory

Decode the instruction

Execute the instruction

Fetching an instruction from memory

In the **fetch** part of the cycle:

Step 1: The address A of the next instruction to be executed is copied from the PC to the Memory Address Register (MAR).

Step 2: The PC is incremented so it points to the next instruction to be fetched.

Simultaneously, the instruction held in location A is then copied into the Memory Data Register (MDR).

Step 3: The contents of the MDR are copied to the Current Instruction Register (CIR).

Decoding and executing an instruction

In the **decode** part of the cycle:

The Control Unit decodes the instruction in the CIR to see what has to be done next.

In the **execute** part of the cycle:

The instruction is executed. Depending on what the instruction is, this could, for example, involve fetching data from memory and loading or adding it into the accumulator or jumping to another instruction in the program.

> Q5
>
> The following instructions are to be carried out.
>
> | Address of instruction | Instruction | Meaning |
> |---|---|---|
> | 23 | LDA #150 | Load value 150 into accumulator |
> | 24 | ADD #1 | Add 1 to contents of accumulator |
> | 25 | STA 60 | Store the result in memory location 60 |
>
> When the computer executes instruction 23, what is held in the CIR? What is held in the PC?
>
> Name two other registers involved in the fetch-execute cycle.

Factors affecting CPU performance

Clock speed

The speed at which a processor operates is quoted as the **clock speed**, and measured in Hertz. Hertz is the name for the number of electrical cycles per second, or the rate at which the electrical current changes in the actual circuits. Everything the processor does occurs on the 'tick' of the clock - so a faster clock means that more instructions are fetched, decoded and executed in a second. One clock cycle per second = 1 Hertz (Hz), and clock speed is measured in Gigahertz (GHz), one billion cycles per second. Typical speeds for a PC are between 2GHz and 4GHz. The greater the clock speed, the faster instructions will be executed.

In theory a computer with a 4GHz processor should operate twice as fast as one with a 2GHz processor, but it isn't that simple. There are many other components that contribute to the overall speed of the computer. Each one can create a bottleneck in the system and slow it down. Imagine a three lane motorway where the traffic can go really fast until it gets to a single lane road going into a town. No matter how many lanes you add to a motorway, the single lane part of the journey will limit how quickly traffic can get into town. In the same way, a slow component can slow the whole computer down.

Type and size of memory

One bottleneck that can occur is the access speed of main memory. Reading from and writing to main memory is much slower than the speed at which the processor can work. The logical answer is to use faster memory technologies but this increases the price of the computer. Modern computers need to run many programs at the same time so they need lots of memory. There needs to be a compromise between speed and cost.

One way of improving speed at minimal cost is to use a small amount of much faster memory where frequently used instructions or data can be stored temporarily. We call this special sort of high-speed memory the **cache** (pronounced "cash").

Cache memory is an intermediary between RAM and the CPU. The cache makes any data frequently used by CPU available much more quickly. Because the processor has to access main memory less often, it can work faster, so the CPU performance increases. If the required information is not located in the cache, it has to be fetched from main memory.

A typical PC (in January 2016) might have 4GB of RAM (main memory) but only 2MB of the faster more expensive cache memory. Notice the different units here and remember that there are 1000 Megabytes in a Gigabyte. This computer therefore has 2000 times more RAM than cache memory.

The more cache memory a computer has, the more data and instructions can be held in cache and made available very quickly. This improves processor performance.

There are different 'levels' of cache:

- **Level 1 cache** is extremely fast but small (between 2-64KB). It is used to hold instructions, thus speeding up the Fetch-Execute cycle
- **Level 2 cache** is fairly fast and medium-sized (256KB-2MB). It is used to hold data
- Some CPUs also have Level 3 data cache

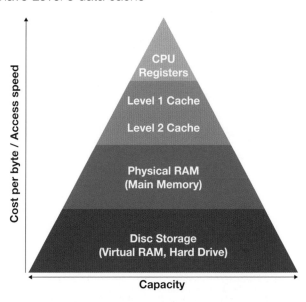

Q6 Explain how clock speed and cache memory can affect the performance of a computer.

Q7 Which type of memory is the most expensive?

Processor cores

When we looked at the basic Fetch-Decode-Execute cycle we assumed that there was a single processor and a single main memory. You have probably heard the terms **dual-core** and **quad-core** so where do these fit in?

Today's more complex CPUs can include more than one core. A dual-core processor has two processing components within the CPU and a quad-core has four. In theory having two processors means that the computer can operate twice as fast but this isn't always the case.

A program is a series of instructions that need to be done in order. Multiple cores could work on different programs that operate in parallel but unless the computer is designed to use multiple cores it isn't necessarily four times faster. On the whole though, a PC with a multi-core processor, executing many tasks at the same time, will operate faster than a single-core processor.

Embedded systems

Many devices in the home use microprocessors/CPUs to control their functions. These are referred to as **embedded systems**. The control devices are usually on a single microprocessor stored within the device. They very often don't need an operating system since the tasks are usually simple and repeated and the input is usually done by pressing a button or setting a control. Examples of items that use this technology include: vehicles, cameras, medical equipment, aircraft, vending machines, ovens, fridges, mobile phones, satellite navigation devices, televisions, clocks and lifts/elevators.

Cockpits contain many embedded systems

The advantages of such technology are that they make devices easier to use whilst also increasing reliability and offering features which enhance their usability.

Many embedded systems can connect to the Internet (usually using a Wi-Fi link) and can exchange data with the manufacturer's website or with the user. These so-called intelligent devices also allow users to set up a satellite box to start recording a television programme or control their central heating system using an App on their smart phone.

Smart meters currently being installed in 26 million homes across Britain measure the gas and electricity you are using and display this on the screen of a handheld device. The smart meters also send automatic meter readings to the energy supplier using wireless technology, so that everyone will get accurate rather than estimated bills every month without any need to read the meter.

1.3 – Memory

Memory and storage devices can be split up into three distinct groups:

- primary memory
- secondary storage
- off-line storage

Off-line storage refers to storage devices which can be stored away from the computer. Secondary storage devices are typically an integral part of the computer.

> **Q8** Name an off-line storage device that is read-only, i.e. cannot be written to.

Random Access Memory (RAM)

RAM is the type of memory used as the computer's main memory. Many people say "RAM" when they mean main memory. Nothing in a computer is really "random" so random access just refers to the fact that you can write anywhere in that memory space at any time. You don't have to put the next thing straight after the last one like you do on a magnetic tape, for example.

When a program is to be executed, it has to be loaded from the hard disk into main memory so that the processor can access the instructions. Any data needed for that program to run is also loaded into main memory. The main purpose of RAM is to act as temporary storage for programs and data while the program is being executed.

So why doesn't the processor get the instructions straight from the hard disk? It is about access speed. Reading from and writing to a hard disk is very slow compared to the speed of the processor. Just as we used the high speed cache between the processor and main memory, we need main memory to store the programs currently being executed or the computer would be really slow.

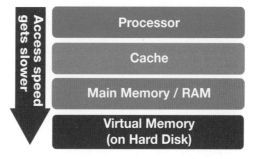

Virtual Memory

Sometimes there just isn't enough main memory to store the whole of a large program, or all the programs which are running at the same time (multi-tasking). Computers can be configured so that part of the hard disk drive (HDD) or solid state drive (SSD) behaves like main memory. This is called **virtual memory**. The access speed on an HDD or SSD is usually slower than the speed of RAM, so this isn't ideal. It is used to store parts of programs currently being run but the parts actually being executed still need to be in main memory. As the processor gets to the next part of the program, sections are swapped between virtual memory and main memory. Sometimes this works well but sometimes the computer spends more time swapping bits around than it does executing the program.

Q9 If this is happening a lot on your computer, what would be the cheapest way to upgrade it?

Volatility

If you are in the middle of a piece of work and you turn off your computer, you will lose the work you did since you last saved. This is because the saved version goes onto the HDD or SSD, but the most recent version was only in RAM when the power went off. RAM is described as **volatile**; it loses its contents if there is no power. HDD and SSD are designed for long term storage of files and are **non-volatile** memory.

Read Only Memory (ROM)

RAM is volatile so when you turn off your computer it loses its contents. When you turn the computer back on it needs to get the basic startup routine from somewhere that is not volatile. The operating system and all your programs will be stored on the HDD/SSD but these need to be loaded into RAM to run.

The computer has a piece of software called the **bootstrap loader**. This is a small program that loads the operating system. Once the operating system is loaded it takes care of the rest. The term comes from the idea that when you're not doing very well in life you can "pull yourself up by your bootstraps". Bootstrapping became abbreviated to booting, a term you have probably heard before. To "boot" a computer is to start it up from scratch.

ROM is **Read Only Memory**; you cannot write over the contents once it has been created. It is also non-volatile; you can leave the computer switched off for months and it will still start up as soon as it has power again. RAM on the other hand is only used for temporary storage of programs when they are running. RAM is read-write and volatile.

RAM	ROM
Volatile – data is lost when the power is turned off (temporary memory)	Non-volatile – data is NOT lost when power is turned off (permanent memory)
Stores user data/programs/part of operating system which is currently in use	Used to store the BIOS/bootstrap loader which is required at start-up of the computer
Memory can be written to or read from	Memory can only be read from and NOT written to

1.4 – Secondary storage

We all want to store files for a long period of time. We keep photographs, projects, music, films, letters and spreadsheets on our computers. We also expect our programs to be there when we switch the computer on. This long term storage is usually called **secondary storage** (primary storage is the main memory). Secondary storage refers to hard disk drives (HDDs) and, more recently, solid state drives (SSDs).

Secondary storage devices

Secondary storage is non-volatile, generally holds much more data than main memory and is relatively inexpensive per MB. However, secondary storage technologies tend to have slower access speeds than main memory.

Secondary storage needs to be robust and reliable. Has your memory stick been through the washing machine yet?

Choosing the right type of storage medium for a particular use is important. You need to consider the following features:

- **Capacity**: How much space there is to store files. A memory stick holding 8GB costs under £10 – how many high-resolution photos each of 10MB can you store on it?
- **Speed**: How quickly can the computer read data from a storage device or write data to it?
- **Portability**: Can you easily unplug it and carry it away? Does it fit in a pencil case or do you need a large bag?
- **Durability**: How easily is it damaged? Will it survive dropping or having coffee tipped on it?
- **Reliability**: How long will it last? Anything with moving parts is likely to be less reliable.
- **Cost**: Storage devices vary in cost per GB.

Magnetic devices

Magnetic disks are read with a moving head inside the disk drive. Moving parts make these media quite slow to read from or write to and also make the disk more susceptible to damage. This is in contrast to solid state media (SSD) which have no moving parts. Magnetic media are also vulnerable to magnetic fields. Just as a credit card with a magnetic strip left on a stereo speaker can be damaged by the magnets, so too a magnetic disk can be wiped by the magnetic fields in speakers.

1

Magnetic disk drives can be either internal or portable (connected to the computer using a USB port).

Although hard disks are less portable than optical or solid state media, their huge capacity makes them very suitable for desktop purposes. Smaller, denser surface areas spinning under the read-write heads mean that newer disks have capacities of several terabytes.

The following table compares both types of hard disk drive:

	Internal Hard Disk	Portable Hard Disk
Physical size	3.5 Inches	2.5 Inches
Cost	3TB for £85	
Capacity	Up to 6TB	Up to 640GB
Access Speed	3Gb/s	480Mb/s (Speed of USB3 interface)
Portability	Not portable, built into PC	Can fit in a large pocket
Durability	Good durability when disk not in use but vulnerable to movement when spinning. Can write to the disk an infinite number of times. Affected by heat and magnetic fields	
Reliability	Extremely reliable	
Typical use	Inside a PC as secondary storage	Supplementary storage for a PC or portable storage where high capacity is required

NOTE: portable hard disk drives are often referred to as off-line storage devices.

Solid State devices

Solid State Drives (SSD) have no moving parts and don't rely on magnetic properties, so are unaffected by magnetic fields. They are often referred to as **flash memory/storage**, but their access speeds are not as fast as RAM.

The main benefits of SSD technology compared to HDD can be summarised as:

- they are more reliable, being less susceptible to shock and damage as they have no moving parts
- they are considerably lighter (which makes them suitable for laptops, tablets and other modern devices)
- they have faster access times than HDDs because they don't spin and data can be accessed instantaneously
- they havelower power consumption
- they run much cooler than HDDs (both these points also make them very suitable for laptop computers)
- because they have no moving parts, they are very thin.

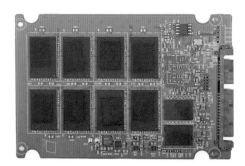

Solid state technology is also used in memory sticks (pen drives) and memory cards (e.g. SD and XD as used in cameras). Solid state technology is now employed in many laptops and tablets as well as in mobile phones, cameras and other portable devices. Small size, non-volatile memory and reliability are key features in such devices which need to be portable and also have minimum drain on the internal batteries.

NOTE: Memory sticks and memory cards are also referred to as off-line storage devices.

	FLASH STORAGE DEVICES		
	Internal Solid State/ Flash Storage	**USB Memory Stick**	**Memory Card**
Cost	128GB for £40 960GB for £200	32GB for £15 128GB for £35	128GB SD card £25
Capacity	128GB to 2TB	16MB to 256GB	2GB to 128GB
Access Speed	6Gb/s (Faster than magnetic disk because no moving parts)	480Mb/s (Speed of USB3 interface)	Dependent on type of card and device interface
Portability	Not portable, built into PC	Very small, can put in a pocket or on a key-ring	Very small, designed for portable devices
Durability	More robust than hard disks with moving parts. Said to be 5-10 times more durable than a hard disk drive	Very durable - some can be snapped quite easily	Very durable - not sensitive to temperature or knocks
Reliability	Extremely reliable	Very reliable but can corrupt files if removed from PC too soon	Very reliable
Typical use	Notebooks, tablets, slim laptops	Personal use, moving files between computers	In phones and cameras

Q10 Which are cheaper, HDDs or SSDs? Is there a big difference in price?

Optical devices

Optical media includes CD, DVD and Blu-Ray disks.

The word "optical" should make you think about the eye and how we see the world in terms of reflected light. Optical media work in a similar way. Lasers write data to the disc and read data from it.

CDs come in three different formats: read-only (CD-ROM), recordable (CD-R) and rewriteable (CD-RW). A CD-ROM is 'pressed' with the data at the time of manufacturing.

Pits and Lands

Spiral track

OPTICAL STORAGE DEVICES		
CD	**DVD**	**Blu-Ray**
Cost 50 x 700MB CD-R for £14 (7p each)	50 x 4.7GB DVD-R for £12 (24p each)	50 x 25GB Blu-ray for £22 (44p each)
Capacity 640MB	4.7GB (single layer) 8.5GB (dual layer)	25GB (single layer) 50GB (dual layer)
Access Speed Up to 7.6 MB/s (52x)	16 MB/s (12x)	50 MB/s (12x)
Portability Easy to carry in a large pocket or bag		
Durability Depends on how it is stored. Quality will degrade over time but the manufacturer's life expectancy is 10 to 25 years. Adversely affected by prolonged exposure to sunlight.		Depends on how it is stored. Quality will degrade over time but the manufacturer's life expectancy is 20 to 100 years
Reliability Good for medium term but degrades over time (still an unknown quantity)		
Typical use CD-ROM for software distribution, CD-R or CD-RW for backup/ archive	DVD is used as a back-up device but also for distribution of software, games and the storage of movies	Blu-ray is used for storing of movies and games but also as a back-up device; very large storage capacity means it is replacing dvds

Cloud storage

Increasingly, users are choosing to store their data and software "in the cloud". Cloud storage refers to saving data in an off-site storage system maintained by a third party, for example Dropbox, Google or Microsoft. Instead of saving data on your computer's hard drive or other local storage device, you save it to a remote storage facility, and access it via the Internet.

There are several advantages to this form of storage:

- You can access the data from anywhere in the world
- You can share the data with other people in different locations
- Backup is no longer such an issue, as it is the responsibility of the provider to keep the data safe

There are also some disadvantages:

- You are dependent on having an Internet connection in order to access your data
- Some users are concerned about security in the cloud, and whether their data could be accessed by a hacker

The data is stored, usually on hard disks but increasingly on solid state drives, in remote locations in different countries.

Google's server room in Council Bluffs, Iowa, USA

Exercises

1. Here are some statements about the CPU of a computer.

   Tick one box in each row to show whether each of the following statements is true or false   [5]

	True	False
CPU stands for Central Processing Unit		
The CPU fetches and decodes instructions		
The speed of the CPU is usually measured in Gigahertz (GHz)		
If a CPU has many cores, this slows down the computer		
The hard disk is part of the CPU		

   OCR A451/01 June 2013 Qu 1

2. (a) Circle the correct options in the following statements about computer architecture:

   (i) Holds the address of the next instruction to be executed.

   CIR   **ALU**   **MAR**   **PC**   [1]

   (ii) Data stored here is not erasable and usually contains instructions for booting the system and other important information.

   ALU   **RAM**   Cache   **ROM**   [1]

   (iii) Arithmetic and logical instructions are carried out here.

   ACC   **MAR**   **ALU**   **CIR**   [1]

3. A computer has 1024 megabytes of RAM.

   (a) How many gigabytes of RAM does the computer have?   [1]

   (b) State **two** items that will be stored in the RAM.   [2]

   (c) The computer sometimes uses virtual memory.
   Describe what is meant by virtual memory and state why it is needed.   [3]

   OCR A451/01 June 2014 Qu 2

4. Mina's computer has 4GB of RAM.

   (a) Describe the purpose of RAM in the computer.   [2]

   (b) The computer also uses virtual memory.

   (i) Explain what is meant by virtual memory.   [2]

   (ii) State why virtual memory is needed.   [1]

   (iii) Mina upgrades the computer to 6GB of RAM.
   Explain how this upgrade will affect the performance of the computer.   [2]

   OCR A451/01 Jan 2012 Qu 8

5. The CPU is the component which does most of the processing in a computer.

   (a) State **two** tasks which are carried out by the CPU when processing data.   [2]

   (b) Explain how the clock speed and the cache size of a CPU affect its performance.   [4]

   OCR A451/01 June 2012 Qu 7

6. State which type of storage device would be most suitable for the following applications. In each case, give a reason why the device is suitable.

    (a) Storing apps on a mobile phone [2]

    (b) Transporting a very large database from one desktop computer to another [2]

    (c) Working collaboratively on the same file with colleagues in a different country. [2]

7. Most computers use at least **one** storage device.

    (a) Explain **one** reason why a secondary storage device is needed in most computer systems. [2]

    (b) Some secondary storage devices are magnetic and others are solid state. Describe the characteristics of magnetic and solid state secondary storage.
    The quality of written communication will be assessed in your answer to this question. [6]

    OCR A451/01 Jan 2013 Qu 4

1

Section 2

Wired and wireless networks

Objectives

- Be familiar with Local and Wide Area Network types

- Understand the factors that affect network performance

- Explain the different roles of computers within client-server and peer-to-peer networks

- Identify and describe the hardware needed to connect stand-alone computers into a LAN:

    o   Wireless access points

    o   Routers and switches

    o   NIC (Network Interface Controller/Card)

    o   Transmission media

- Understand that the Internet is a worldwide collection of computer networks

- Describe what is meant by:

    o   DNS (Domain Name Server)

    o   Hosting

    o   The cloud

- Explain the concept of virtual networks

- Describe mesh and star network topologies

- Explain Wi-Fi, frequency and channels, and encryption

- Understand the uses of IP addressing and MAC addressing

- Describe different protocols including TCP/IP, HTTP, HTTPS, FTP, POP, IMAP, SMTP

Describe the concept of layers

Describe packet switching

2.1 – The Internet

An introduction to the Internet

The Internet is a worldwide collection of **Inter**-connected **net**works, not owned or managed by any one group of people. Anyone can access the Internet.

The Internet is not the same thing as the World Wide Web. Websites are stored on web servers connected to the Internet, and each site has a unique web address so that it can be accessed. All information on the World Wide Web is stored in documents known as **web pages**. These pages are accessed using a program called a **web browser** such as Firefox, Mozilla or Google Chrome.

The Web is just one of the ways in which information is communicated over the Internet. The Internet, not the Web, is used for email and instant messaging.

How does a message travelling from one computer to another halfway round the world find the correct destination?

IP addressing

Every networked computer or computing device in the world has a separate, unique **IP address**, although you will see later that a mobile device's IP address changes as it moves location. The current addressing system is called IPv4. IP stands for **Internet Protocol** and an IP version 4 address takes the form:

$$65.123.217.14$$

However, it is predicted that by 2020, more than 50 billion devices will be connected to the Internet and we will run out of addresses, so a new system IPv6 is replacing IPv4.

Domain names

Websites are stored on web servers connected to the Internet. Each website has an IP address so people can access the pages using their browser software. However, when you want to access a site you don't enter the IP address, you type in a **domain name** such as **www.rspb.org.uk** This is because humans are quite bad at remembering numbers and typing them in correctly, so the domain name is a text reference to a site that can be translated into the numerical IP address.

The Domain Name System (DNS)

When you type the domain name **www.rspb.org.uk** into the browser the web page request is sent to a **Domain Name System (DNS)** server on the Internet. The DNS server has a database of domain names and IP addresses so it can translate the domain name into an IP address.

There is a large number of DNS servers across the globe and these communicate with each other so the DNS servers are regularly updated. If your local DNS server does not have the domain name listed, the page request is forwarded to another DNS server.

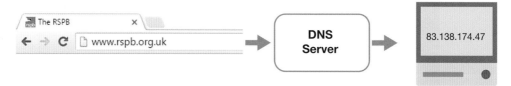

The advantages of using DNS servers to translate domain names into IP addresses are:

- Humans do not have to remember or type in numerical addresses
- If the IP addresses change at some point the DNS servers can update their databases, and the users can continue using the same domain names
- Having many distributed DNS servers means that everyone has access to all addresses from their local DNS server

In most browsers you can also type the IP address into the address bar to get to a site. Although you would not normally do this, it shows that essentially the domain name and IP address both address the same place. This IP address gets you to the RSPB home page:

The IP address is used to give the **location** of the device connected to the network/Internet. Each time a device connects to a network/Internet, it is allocated a unique IP address by a user's ISP. This means that as you move around with your mobile phone, its IP address will change every time you move across an invisible network boundary.

MAC addressing

In order to connect to the Internet, a computer device must have a piece of hardware called a **Network Interface Controller/card (NIC)**. Each NIC has a Media Access Control or **MAC address** assigned to it by the manufacturer. Your computer may have more than one MAC address – one for wired **Ethernet** and one for **wireless**. A mobile phone may have different MAC addresses for wireless and **Bluetooth**.

A MAC address is a 48-bit address that is written as twelve hex digits to make it easier for humans to work with. The first six digits (e.g. 00-1C-B3) are used to identify the manufacturer of the device – in this case, Apple Corporation. The second set of digits gives the serial number of the device. For example:

In hex: **00-1C-B3-F1-F7-85**

In binary: 0000 0000 0001 1100 1011 0011 1111 0001 1111 0111 1000 0101

This is the MAC address of a device with serial number F1-F7-85 made by Apple.

Every networked device in the world has a unique, unchanging MAC address.

Q1 Why doesn't the Internet use a MAC address instead of an IP address to locate a networked device on the Internet?

Wide Area Networks

The Internet is the largest and most famous Wide Area Network in the world. But some large and medium-sized organisations have their own private Wide Area Networks, or WANs. A WAN is a collection of computers and networks connected together using resources supplied by a "third party carrier" such as British Telecom. It uses cables, telephone lines, satellites and radio waves to connect the components, which are usually spread over a wide geographical area.

A business with offices in London, Leeds, Bristol and York may lease connections from a network service provider to connect the four office LANs together.

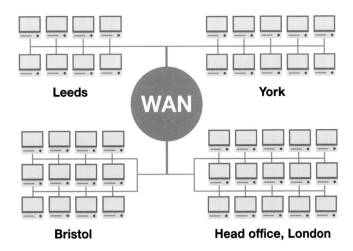

Leeds   WAN   York

Bristol   Head office, London

Circuit switching and packet switching

When you make a telephone call, a dedicated connection is set up between you and the person you are calling for the duration of the call. This is called **circuit switching**. This is fine for telephone calls, but there could never be enough lines for all the billions of people sending data across the Internet.

This is where **packet switching** comes in.

Suppose you want to send a file of 3MB across the Internet. The file is broken up into data 'packets' of around 512 bytes. Each packet is given a header containing:

- The IP (Internet Protocol) address it is going to
- The IP address it has come from
- The sequence number of the packet
- The number of packets in the whole communication
- Error checking data

Packets are then sent to their destination along different routes, and reassembled in the right order when they arrive.

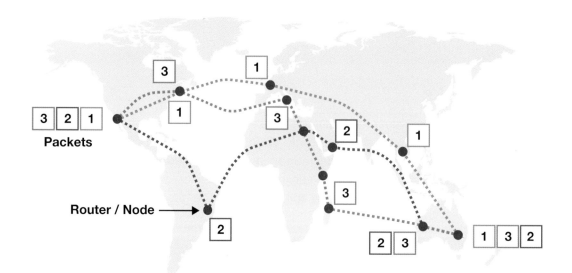

2

2.2 – Local Area Networks

Local Area Networks (LANs)

A **Local Area Network (LAN)** usually covers a relatively small geographical area. It consists of a collection of computers and peripheral devices (such as printers) connected together, often on a single site. At school you probably have many different buildings within a campus, with the school's LAN connecting the computers in all these buildings. A LAN is often owned and managed by a single person or organisation.

Benefits of Networking Computers

These are some of the benefits of networking computers belonging to a single organisation:

Sharing resources

- folders and files can be stored on a file server so they can be accessed by authorised users from any computer on the network
- peripheral devices such as printers and scanners can be shared
- Internet connection can be shared and any authorised user on the network can use email

Centralised management

- user profiles and security can all be managed centrally
- software can be distributed across the network rather than having to install it on each individual computer
- all files can be backed up centrally

The disadvantages of networking computers include network administration and security:

- Managing a large network is complicated
- Viruses may be able to infiltrate the network and infect every computer

Network Topologies

Computers can be connected together in different layouts, or **topologies**. Two common topologies are **star** and **mesh**.

Star networks

All of the computers have their own cable connecting them to a **switch**, which routes messages to the correct computer. A powerful computer called the **server** controls the network.

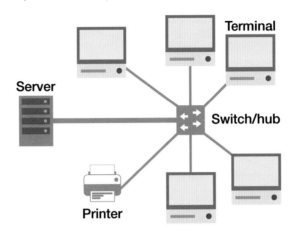

Advantages:	Disadvantages:
If one cable fails the other workstations are not affected	Can be costly to install because there is a lot of cabling and extra hardware e.g. a switch
Consistent performance even when the network is heavily used	If the server or the central switch fails then the whole network goes down

Mesh networks

A **mesh network** can be a local area network (LAN), a wireless LAN (WLAN) or a virtual LAN (see below). Wireless mesh networks are an emerging technology, which can connect small offices or entire cities.

In a wireless mesh network, there is no central connection point. Instead, each point on the network acts as a 'node', equipped with a small radio transmitter. Information travels from node A to node B by hopping wirelessly from one mesh node to another, choosing the quickest route.

To connect to the Internet, only one node needs to be physically connected via a **modem**. This node shares its connection with all the other nodes close to it. These nodes then share the connection with the nodes closest to them, and so on. The more nodes, the further the connection spreads, creating a wireless network that can serve a small office or a city of millions.

Case Study: Doncaster Council

Doncaster has 33,000 streetlights connected in a wireless mesh network. The communications system uses nodes attached to the streetlights to control them - which in turn communicate with electronic base stations up to five miles away. The authorities can manipulate the lights as they want, for example dimming lights in certain areas between 10pm and 5am, and they can instantly identify non-working streetlights from the base station.

Each node costs £45 and the Council expects to save about £1.3m per year.

In a **full mesh network**, each node is connected to every other node.

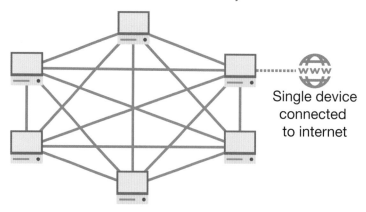

Single device
connected
to internet

In a partial mesh network, some nodes are not directly connected.

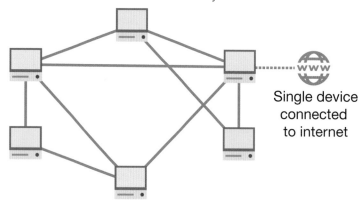

Single device
connected
to internet

The advantages of wireless mesh networks include:

- Using fewer cables means it costs less to set up a network, particularly over a large area of coverage
- The more nodes that are installed, the bigger and faster the wireless network becomes
- New nodes are automatically incorporated into the network without needing any adjustments by a network administrator
- Even if one node is blocked or faulty, the network will automatically 'self-heal' to find another route to send messages from one computer to another
- Local networks run faster because local packets don't have to travel back to a central switch or server

Network hardware

The hardware required to create a network of computers includes **routers**, **switches** and **Network Interface Cards (NICs)**. Cabling and wireless access points may also be required and these are covered later in this section.

Routers and switches

A **router** is designed to route data packets across a wide area network such as the Internet. Each router in a network acts as a node and packets are passed from router to router to their destination somewhere on the Internet. If a packet is destined for a computer in a LAN, it will typically be routed to a **switch**.

A **switch** is a component of a LAN that knows the MAC addresses of each individual device connected to it locally. Its function is to forward the inbound packets only to the intended recipient, using its MAC address.

Network Interface Card (NIC)

A **Network Interface Card (NIC)** is required to connect any network-enabled device. This is a physical component which can either operate wirelessly or have a wired connection using a standard Ethernet cable. All devices that can connect to a network have an NIC including your home computer, a smartphone, an Internet-enabled light bulb or a network printer.

A Network Interface Card

Ethernet

Ethernet refers to a family of networking rules or prototocols widely used in Local Area Networks.

It describes how devices should format data ready for transmission between computers on the same network.

- Similar to polite human conversation, nodes will wait until the connection is quiet before attempting to 'speak' or transmit
- Two nodes attempting to transmit simultaneously will stop and each wait a random period before reattempting

Ethernet systems divide data into frames, similar to Internet packets. Each frame contains source and destination MAC addresses and error checking data. Faulty frames containing transmission errors are dropped or resent. All new computers have Ethernet built in, and old machines can be retro-fitted. Almost every reference to "network ready," "LAN" or "LAN connection" implies use of the Ethernet system.

2

Transmission media

The standard network cable is often referred to as an Ethernet cable. It uses twisted-pair copper cabling or fibre optics.

Selecting cable types

Connecting computers with copper cable is cheaper, as most PCs come with built-in copper Network Interface Cards (NICs). Optical NICs cost around £100 each.

Copper cable offers advantages in rural areas where it may already be used in telephone networks. Using the existing cable will save the cost of running new cable throughout a site for a LAN. For most applications the speed of copper cable is adequate so the lower associated cost of NICs and routing equipment mean it is widely used, especially in LANs.

However, in many situations fibre optic is the cable of choice. It has much greater bandwidth, transmission is faster and the cables do not break as easily as copper cables. They are not affected by electromagnetic interference, unlike copper cables which can interfere with other wires and cause lost or distorted transmissions over a network. Over a distance of 100 metres, fibre optic cable loses only 3% of signal strength, whereas copper cable loses 94% over the same distance and will need repeaters or boosters above that distance.

Virtual networks

A **virtual network** is a subset of computers connected together as part of a larger physical network. The computers identified as part of the virtual network act as a smaller private network. A **Virtual Private Network** (**VPN**) can be set up when an employee of a company in a remote location needs to connect to the company's private network. Communications may be encrypted for security purposes and to prevent network users of the wider physical network from being able to access data being transmitted within the VPN. A school may use a VPN to provide a private network for staff that students cannot access, even though the student machines are also part of the same physical network.

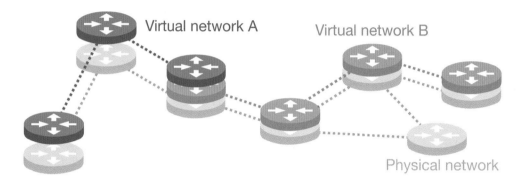

Q2 Are you able to connect to the school network when you are working from home? If so, you are using a virtual private network.

2.3 – Wireless networking

Wi-Fi

Many networks use wireless fidelity (**Wi-Fi**) connections rather than physical wires. Like Ethernet, Wi-Fi is also a family of protocols or rules that make wireless networking run smoothly.

Wireless Access Points (WAPs)

A wireless transmitter (**Wireless Access Point – WAP**) receives data from a network via its physical connection. The transmitter then converts this data into radio waves which are then transmitted. Any device on the network receives this radio signal via a Wi-Fi adaptor which allows it to communicate or download data from the data source. As you might expect, this also works in the reverse direction when a device wishes to send data over the network to another computer.

Risks of wireless networking

A typical network will have **hot spots** around a WAP where it is possible for any device to gain illicit Wi-Fi access to the network. Risks include:

- Criminal activity – wireless networks are often connected to in-house private networks. This may allow an intruder to completely bypass any hardware firewall protective devices between the private network and the broadband connection. An unauthorised user can use the wireless connection to hack into the network and cause damage by planting viruses or launching Denial of Service attacks.

- Bandwidth stealing – by using the Internet connection to download music, games and other software, outside intruders can slow the network down and reduce employee productivity

- Confidentiality – if any network information is not encrypted before transmission, an intruder can gain access to confidential information

Wireless security and encryption

Wi-Fi poses more security risks than wired data transmission, since most devices (computers, tablets and smartphones) can 'see' all the Wi-Fi hot spots within range. There are a number of security measures to protect against any device not authorised to access this network:

- Disabling broadcast of the Service Set IDentifier (SSID), thus hiding the network from opportunists looking to connect to a named local network

- Restricting access to only certain MAC addresses

- Using Wi-Fi protected access (WPA) encryption to prevent data and signals being read by an outsider

Wi-Fi frequencies and channels

Almost all Wi-Fi installations use the 2.4GHz or the 5GHz band, operating at frequencies of 2.4GHz or 5GHz respectively. These frequencies are subdivided into several overlapping channels, each with a central frequency and bandwidth. If, for example, you are using Channel 1 and your neighbour starts to use Channel 2, an overlapping band, the performance of your network will drop.

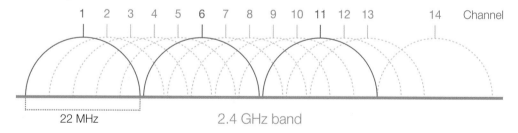

On most routers, the **channel** is set to Auto, but there is a choice of a dozen or so channels, and some will transmit data faster than others.

	Advantages	**Disadvantages**
2.4GHz	Greater range and coverage	More interference from other devices, and only three non-overlapping channels
5GHz	Less crowded space with 23 non-overlapping channels and higher data transmission rates	Fewer devices can use the 5GHz frequency, less able to penetrate through walls

Encryption

Encryption is used primarily to protect data in case it has been hacked or accessed illegally. Data that is being transmitted over the Internet is vulnerable to hackers. For example, someone who uses an online shopping site will have to type in their payment details, such as a credit or debit card number, and it is essential that this information is kept secure. If they are paying by PayPal, they will have to type in their email address and password, which needs to be kept safe from anyone intercepting the transmission.

Whilst encryption won't prevent hacking, it makes the data unreadable unless the recipient has the necessary decryption tools.

Encryption terminology

- **Plaintext**: the original message to be encrypted

- **Ciphertext**: the encrypted message

- **Encryption**: the process of converting plaintext into ciphertext

- **Key**: a sequence of numbers used to encrypt or decrypt, often using a mathematical formula

- **Encryption algorithm**: the method for encrypting the plaintext

Symmetric encryption

Symmetric encryption uses a secret key which can be a combination of letters, numbers and other characters. A single key is used to encrypt and decrypt a message and must be given to the recipient of your message so that they can decrypt and read it.

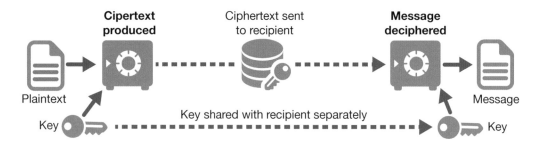

A very simple example of symmetric encryption is the Caesar shift cipher, in which each letter is replaced by a letter n number of positions further on in the alphabet. The key in this case is 3:

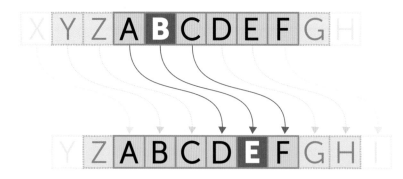

Q3 Given the key 5, decode the encrypted message KNWJHWFHPJW BNQQ QTXJ

Asymmetric encryption

There are a number of risks with symmetric encryption; particularly if the encryption key falls into the wrong hands. A more secure method is to use asymmetric or public key encryption. With this system, a private key and a public key are both needed. Initially User A receives a public key and a private key pair from a certificate authority. User B, wanting to send an encrypted message to User A, uses the public key sent to them by User A. User A then decrypts the message using their private key, which is not shared with anyone else.

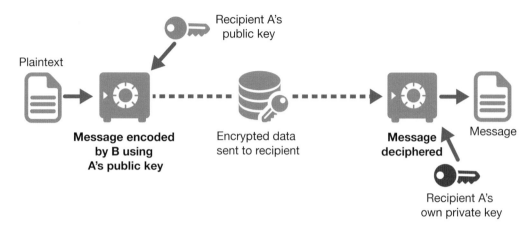

2.4 – Client-server and peer-to-peer networks

Client-server networks

In your school you will be able to use your files on computers in different buildings. This is because they are not stored on the computer that you are using but are on a **file server** somewhere else in school. The server is a specialised computer with a different role from the normal PC. There will probably be a **web server** to host the school's external website and an **email server** which receives all emails and distributes them to network users. It may detect and block incoming emails that it thinks are spam.

In a large network it is common to have shared files and resources on centralised servers. The computers that you use around school are referred to as **clients**.

In a client-server network:

- The **server** is a powerful computer which provides services or resources required by any of the clients
- A **client** is a computer which requests the services or resources provided by the server

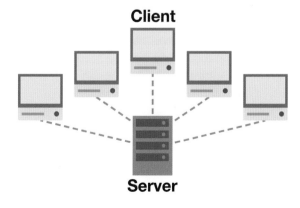

Peer-to-peer configuration

In smaller offices with a handful of computers, it is not practical or cost-effective to have a specialised server or someone to run the network. The computers will simply be cabled or wirelessly connected together. Each computer is configured so it will share specified files and folders with other peer computers on the LAN. PCs on the LAN can only access files on another computer if access rights have been granted. This is called a peer-to-peer network because all of the computers have equal status and the same role in the network.

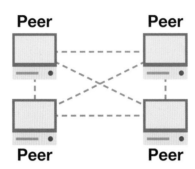

Client-Server	Peer-to-Peer
A central backing store is available to all computers	Storage facilities are distributed across all computers
Security is controlled by the central computer	Security is not centrally controlled
Backup is done centrally on the server	Backup must be done separately for each computer
All users are reliant on the central server	No central server
Can support hundreds or even thousands of users and grow with an organisation	Easy to set up but most suited to homes and small businesses

Hosting

An Internet host is a company (often an ISP) that is able to store your files and make them available to you or others from other Internet-connected computers

These include:

- Website pages, images and related files
- Online file hosting services such as OneDrive or DropBox
- Video hosting services such as YouTube

When a company or individual wants to have their own website, they need a web hosting service to make the website accessible on the World Wide Web. Web hosting often includes **domain name registration** which ensures that the name chosen for the website has not already been taken, and if it is acceptable, is then registered on a Domain Name Server.

The files making up the web pages can be uploaded to the host's server using the **File Transfer Protocol (FTP)**. Many Internet Service Providers such as BT, Virgin Media or Sky offer this service free to subscribers.

Large companies may have their own dedicated web server.

Cloud storage

Cloud storage is a method of data storage where data and software is stored on offsite web servers – the physical storage can cover literally hundreds of servers in many locations worldwide. The physical environment is owned and managed by a web hosting company which is responsible for keeping the data available and accessible. More detail on cloud storage can be found in Section 1.4.

 Q4 Instead of saving data on a local hard disk or other storage device, a user can save their data "in the Cloud". What are the benefits and drawbacks of storing your data in the Cloud?

Cloud-based servers enable access to software on demand, typically on a subscription basis.

Instead of having the software installed on a local machine, you can access the software (including mobile phone applications) from any Internet-connected computer.

Factors affecting network performance

Bandwidth is the main factor affecting network performance. Bandwidth is measured in megabits per second (Mbps), and the higher the bandwidth, the faster data is transferred.

Latency is the time delay between the moment that transmission of the first byte or packet of a communication starts, and when it is received at its destination. It is a function of the time it takes the information to travel at the speed of light from source to destination. When satellite links are involved, distances of more than 100,000 km are involved and you can sometimes see the result on live TV when a presenter in a studio talks to a reporter at a distant location.

Errors in transmission due to noise or distortion mean that the data has to be retransmitted.

2.5 – Protocols and layers

Protocols

If one computer transmits a stream of binary to another computer, the receiving end needs to know what the rules are. This is called a **protocol**. A protocol is the set of rules that define how devices communicate. A protocol will specify, for example:

- the format of data packets
- the addressing system
- the transmission speed
- error-checking procedures being used

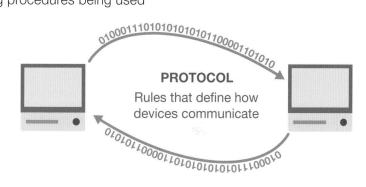

Transmission Control Protocol / Internet Protocol (TCP/IP)

TCP/IP consists of two separate protocols. **TCP** is a standard that defines how messages are broken up into packets and reassembled at the destination. It also detects errors and resends lost packets. The **IP** protocol identifies the location of a device on the Internet and routes the individual packets from source to destination via routers.

HyperText Transfer Protocol (HTTP) and HyperText Transfer Protocol Secure (HTTPS)

HTTP (HyperText Transfer Protocol) is used for accessing and receiving web pages in the form of HTML (Hypertext Markup Language) files on the Internet. The protocol requests the web server to transmit the requested web page to the user's browser for viewing.

HTTPS (Secure protocol) encrypts the information so that it cannot be understood if it is hacked. Banks always use the https protocol.

> **Q5** What other websites might require the use of https?

File Transfer Protocol (FTP)

This is a standard network protocol used when transferring computer files between a client and server on a computer network. **FTP** is based on a client-server model and uses separate control and data connections between the client and the server.

Email protocols

Mail servers pass on or store emails until they are collected. You must log on to a mail server to collect mail.

Post Office Protocol (POP)

This is a widespread method of receiving email. Much like the physical version of a post office clerk, **POP** receives and holds email for an individual until they pick it up. Periodically, you will check your mailbox on the server and download any mail, probably using POP. Since POP creates local copies of emails and deletes the originals from the server, the emails are tied to that specific device.

Internet Messaging Access Protocol (IMAP)

The Internet Message Access Protocol (**IMAP**) is an email protocol that stores email messages on a server but allows users to view and manipulate the messages as though they were stored locally on their own computers. Users can organise messages into folders, flag messages as urgent and save draft messages on the server. While the POP protocol assumes that your email is being accessed from only one application, IMAP allows simultaneous access by multiple clients. This is why IMAP is more suitable for you if you're going to access your email from different devices or if your messages are managed by multiple users.

POP	IMAP
Works best with only one computer to check your email	You can use multiple computers and devices to check your email.
Your emails are downloaded and stored on the computer that you use	Your emails are stored on the server and your devices synchronise with the server.
Sent email is stored locally on your computer and not on an email server.	Sent email stays on the server so you can access it from any device.

Simple Mail Transfer Protocol (SMTP)

SMTP is a protocol for sending e-mail messages between servers. Most e-mail systems that send mail over the Internet use SMTP to send messages from one server to another; this is necessary if the sender and recipient have different email service providers. The messages can then be retrieved with an e-mail client using either POP or IMAP. Users typically use a program that uses SMTP for sending e-mail and either POP or IMAP for receiving e-mail.

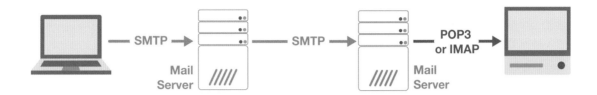

The concept of layers

The TCP/IP model consists of four layers, creating a modular design with each layer responsible for a small part of the communication process.

The advantage of this modular design is that it lets suppliers such as Microsoft easily adapt the protocol software to specific hardware and operating systems. For example, software for an Ethernet system can be adapted to an optical-fibre network by changing only the network layer – other layers are not affected.

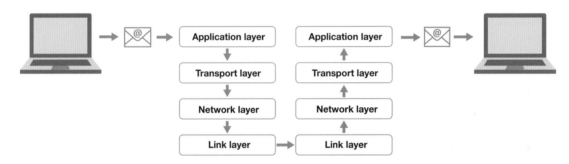

- At the top there is the **Application layer** which encodes the data being sent so that it will be understandable by the recipient. This means formatting data and adding an appropriate header according to a protocol being used, such as HTTP or FTP.
- Next there is the **Transport layer** which splits the data into packets and adds packet information such as packet number specifying that packet's order and the total number of packets so they can be reassembled correctly.
- The third layer is the **Network/Internet Layer** which attaches the IP address of the sender so the recipient will know who sent it. It also attaches the address of the host that is sending the data, and the destination IP address.
- The fourth layer is the **Link layer** which attaches the MAC addresses of the sender and the recipient, allowing the packet to be directed to a specific device on a local area network, for example.

At the receiving end, these data packets are passed back up the protocol stack.

 If the device receiving a communication via the Internet is part of a mesh network, which destination IP address will be added to the packet in the Network/Internet Layer? (Tip: Look back at the diagram of a mesh network.)

Exercises

1. A small company with five employees has installed a Local Area Network (LAN).

    (a) Describe what is meant by a Local Area Network (LAN). [2]

    (b) The network has been connected using a star topology.
        Describe the star topology. You may use a diagram. [2]

    (c) State **one** other item of hardware that is needed to connect stand-alone computers in a LAN, and briefly describe its purpose. [2]

    (d) Give **two** advantages and **one** disadvantage of connecting standalone computers in a LAN. [3]

2. A retailer store has 20 stores in different parts of the country. Each store has a LAN that connects checkout tills and computers used for stock control and administrative purposes.
    Each store is connected to the Head Office where the main servers are located.
    Compare the use of a wide area network (WAN) and a virtual private network (VPN) and state with reasons which would be the most suitable for the company. [6]

3. (a) Describe, with the aid of a diagram, the essential features of a mesh network. [3]

    (b) Give **three** advantages of a wireless mesh network. [3]

4. Explain the purpose of

    (a) an IP address [2]

    (b) a MAC address [2]

    (c) When data is sent from one computer to another across the Internet, the data is split up into **packets**.
        Give **four** items that will be included in each packet in addition to the data. [4]

5. (a) Explain the function of a **hosting service** in the context of the Internet, giving an example. [3]

    (b) Explain what is meant by **Cloud storage** and give **one** advantage of using it. [2]

6. (a) When two computers on a network communicate, they have to use the same **protocol**. What is meant by a protocol? [2]

    (b) State **three** items that may be included in a transmission protocol. [3]

    (c) State which would be the most suitable protocol in each of the following situations. Select **one** in each case, from the following:

               TCP/IP   HTTP   HTTPS   FTP   POP   IMAP   SMTP

        (i) Making a payment securely when purchasing something over the Internet [1]

        (ii) Transferring a file to another computer on a wide area network [1]

        (iii) Transferring an email from one mail server to another mail server [1]

    (d) Sensitive data may be **encrypted** before being transmitted to prevent a hacker from being able to read it. Using a simple Caesar cipher, in which each letter is replaced by a letter further along in the alphabet, the word FUN may be encrypted as GVO.

        Using a shift key of 3, write the word **FLY** in ciphertext. [1]

7. The TCP/IP protocol is commonly used when transmitting data across the Internet. It consists of four **layers**.

    (a) Explain the concept of layers. [2]

    (b) Name and explain the function of **two** of the layers in a layered protocol. [4]

    (c) What is the advantage of layering? [2]

2

Section 3

Systems software and security

Objectives

- Understand forms of attack and threats to a network
    - malware
    - phishing
    - people as the 'weak point' in secure systems (social engineering)
    - brute force attacks
    - denial of service attacks
    - data interception and theft
    - the concept of SQL injection
    - poor network policy

- Identify and explain ways to prevent vulnerabilities
    - penetration testing
    - network forensics
    - network policies
    - anti-malware software
    - firewalls
    - user access levels
    - passwords
    - encryption

- Describe the purpose and functions of an operating system
    - user interface
    - memory management / multitasking
    - peripheral management and drivers
    - user management
    - file management

- Describe the purpose and functions of common utility programs
    - encryption software
    - defragmentation
    - data compression

- Describe the role and methods of backup
    - full
    - incremental

3.1 – Network threats

Security is about keeping your computer and the files, programs and data stored on it safe from a number of hazards. These hazards come in the form of malware, hackers, blagging, phishing, pharming, hardware and software faults. Other users on networks can also be one of the biggest risks of all.

Malware

Viruses are a form of **malware**.

A virus is a program that is installed on a computer without your knowledge or permission with the purpose of doing harm. It includes instructions to replicate (copy itself) automatically on a computer and between computers.

Some viruses are just annoying and don't do any damage but others will delete and/or change system files so that work files are corrupted or the computer becomes unusable. Some viruses fill up the hard drive/SSD so that your computer runs very slowly or becomes unresponsive.

How are viruses spread?

- Viruses are often spread though attachment to emails or instant messaging services. You may be invited to open a funny image, greetings card, audio or video file.

- They may also be spread through files, programs or games that you download from a web page or by loading an infected file from a memory stick or a CD/DVD.

> **Q1** Can a CD or DVD containing games software, bought new from a reputable manufacturer, contain a virus? Why is this unlikely?

3

Phishing

Phishing emails are designed to steal money, get login details, or steal an identity. You may receive an email inviting you to click on a link to download a free game or verify your bank account details. The criminal will then ask you to enter data such as a bank account number or password as well as personal details such as name, address, birth date and so on.

Halifax Bank Plc (no-reply@home.ne.jp)
To: recipients

Hi,

We're just checking this is the right email address for you.

Soon your email address will become your username to access Halifax Account - that makes it easier than remembering yet another username.

If this is the email address you want to use, all you have to do is click the link below

https://my.halifax.co.uk/your-account/verify-email-details?verificationCode=eee96442-51d6-4868-b0f3-a5484447eae8

You should always beware of links in emails! The email is usually not addressed to you personally and often contains spelling and grammar mistakes. Sometimes it contains a threat that something bad will happen if you don't click on the link, for example, your account will be closed down in two days' time.

Once a hacker has your email address, they may have access to your contact list and so they can email your friends pretending to be you. The email may be an urgent request for your help:

CraigWilson (craigwilson@gmail.com)
To: jjdawes@aol.com

Sorry for any inconvenience, I'm in a terrible situation. Am stranded here in Ukrein since last night. I was beaten and robbed on my way to the hotel I stayed and my luggage is still in custody of the hotel management pending when I make payment on outstanding bills I owe. Am waiting for my colleague to send me money to get back home but he hasn't responded. please let me know if you can help and I will refund the money back to you as soon as I get back home. My return flight will be leaving soon, please let me know if I can count on you..

Craig

Q2 Describe one other way you might recognise a "phishing" email. How can you protect yourself from falling for a phishing attack?

Human error

3

People are often the weakest point in security systems and criminals have engineered methods to take advantage of human error and gullibility. Many IT rules do not take into account the frailty of human nature. System users often don't believe that security rules refer to them in their everyday use of computer systems.

Case Study

In one study carried out, researchers scattered several memory sticks and floppy disks in the car parks of a number of companies. Nearly 60% of workers who found these devices used them in their office computers without giving any consideration to potential security risks. The percentage of workers who used these devices actually rose to 90% when they saw an official logo printed on the device.

Human error is by far one of the largest single factors in security breaches. For example, in 2010 GCHQ lost 35 laptops with all the security data stored on these devices; there are numerous similar cases reported on the internet.

Even the use of passwords is no guarantee of security. On average, Internet users have about 25 applications or devices (e.g. phones and tablets) that they have to manage; research has shown that these users often only have five or six unique passwords covering all devices and applications.

It is important that managers of staff using computers are aware of these shortcomings and take the necessary action.

Blagging

Blagging is the act of "knowingly or recklessly obtaining or disclosing personal data or information without the consent of the controller" (owner of the data). For example, a dishonest employee may persuade a colleague to tell them private information such as their password, pretending that they need it in order to install some new software on their computer.

This then gives them access to their computer files and could lead to a security breach or even identity theft.

To prevent blagging, the company should make sure that they provide **security training** to their employees so that they don't fall for these tricks.

This, of course, could also be used on social networking sites where people are tricked into giving out personal data which could lead to all kinds of problems.

> **Q3** "A private detective at the centre of allegations that computers were hacked for the News of the World has been jailed for illegal 'blagging'."
>
> Discuss this story from a daily newspaper. Why do you think the newspaper may have allowed blagging by one of its reporters?

Hacking

There are many ways in which a hacker may try to get access to confidential information. One way is to try and discover the correct password.

Brute force attacks

A **brute force attack** refers to an attack that goes through a list of different passwords or letters until access to an account is eventually gained.

A simple brute-force attack may use a dictionary of all commonly used passwords and cycle through those passwords until it finally gains access to the account. A more complex brute-force attack involves trying every possible key combination (i.e. the letters, numbers and symbols found on a typical keyboard) until the correct password is finally found.

> **Q4** What is the best protection against a brute-force attack?

You can try out the effectiveness of your password on a website such as http://www.howsecureismypassword.net

Denial of Service (DoS) attacks

Denial of Service (DoS) attacks are an attempt to prevent legitimate users from accessing a website. One of the methods used is to flood a company's network with useless traffic. The network will soon become overloaded and can 'crash' or appear to be unresponsive.

An individual user may also be affected by an attacker sending out millions of spam messages to their email account. Since their Internet Service Provider (ISP) will only allow a finite amount of storage, this means their account will quickly become full thus preventing legitimate emails from reaching their account. It is possible to minimise these effects by using virus checkers, firewalls (which restrict traffic entering a user's computer) or applying email filters.

Data interception and theft

All of the above security risks are remote theft. But there are other ways to gain unauthorised access to passwords and confidential material. **Shouldering** means looking over someone's shoulder while they type in the PIN or password. Gaining access to a computer that has been left logged in by the user when they go to lunch is another technique.

These are some of the measures that can be taken to prevent data theft:

* Destroy paper documents once they are no longer needed or file them away in a secure place

* If a user has to step out of the office, then their computer should be logged off or the computer locked out to prevent unauthorised use

* If possible, lock the room containing the computer as an additional precaution

Poor network policy

Some of these security problems can be attributed to a poor network policy. Employees need to be given strict guidelines about what is and is not acceptable behaviour in relation to information technology and its use. Network policy will be considered further in the next section.

> **Q5** Make three suggestions that you think should be included on an Acceptable Use Policy for the use of computer hardware and software at work, to help maintain privacy and security.

SQL injection

SQL (Structured Query Language) injection is a technique that exploits security weaknesses in a website. It achieves this by inserting malicious code into a database field on a website. Such attacks can be used to corrupt or disable targeted websites, or spread viruses and other malware. They may also be designed to steal information such as credit card numbers, Social Security numbers, passwords or other personal or sensitive data. SQL injection is one of the most dangerous and well-known security vulnerabilities on the Internet.

Here is a simple example. Suppose the following code has been created to allow a user to make a database query. The records in the database are very sensitive, so the system is set up to require a *Username* and a *Password* from a list of stored *Usernames* and *Passwords* before access can be granted:

```
SELECT *
FROM usersList
WHERE (Username = $username)
AND (Password = $password);
```

A user will run this query by inputting a `Username` and a `Password`. An interpreter (see Section 7.4) will execute the above code using the input supplied by the user. If the `Username` and `Password` match up with those in the `usersList` then the user will be allowed to access the database files.

However, if a hacker enters "`$username) OR (1=1`" as their User ID and "`$password) OR (1=1`" as their password, the code is injected with additional conditions as follows:

```
SELECT *
FROM usersList
WHERE (Username = $username) OR (1=1)
AND (Password = $password) OR (1=1);
```

The interpreter will accept Username and Password from the normal list or when 1=1. Since it is **always** true that 1=1, the hacker will now be able to see all the records in the database thus leading to a major breach in security.

It is possible to take steps to guard against this potentially serious security breach by:

* checking the parameters used in the SQL query to make sure they follow a strict pattern
* limiting permissions to use the database by setting **access levels**

3.2 – Identifying and preventing vulnerabilities

Vulnerability of a computer network is often due to a flawed system which is open to attack. An attacker or hacker can then exploit this weakness.

Identifying vulnerabilities

There are some methods a company can use to identify vulnerabilities. These include:

* network forensics
* penetration testing

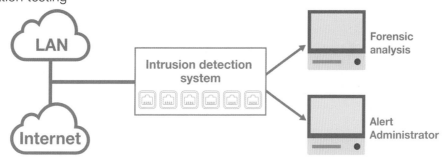

Network forensics

In police work, forensics often involves the use of scientific methods and techniques in investigating a crime. The term is applied in a similar way in the context of network forensics. It involves capturing, storing and analysing network events.

Using special software, network managers can look at business transactions to verify that they are not fraudulent, or stop a security attack before it brings the network to a grinding halt. It can also detect data leaks, where confidential data is going to an external source.

Network forensics can reveal who communicated with whom, when, how, and how often.

Penetration Testing

Penetration testing is used to find any security weaknesses in a system. The strategy is to:

- gather information about the target of possible attacks
- identify possible entry points
- attempt to break in
- report back the findings

An **external penetration test** could target e-mail servers, web servers or firewalls. The objective is to find out whether a hacker can get in and, once they're in, how far they can get and what they can do on the system.

An **internal penetration test** puts the tester in the position of an employee with standard access rights, to determine how much damage a disgruntled or dishonest employee could cause.

> **Q6** Name some possible weaknesses or vulnerabilities that (a) an external penetration test and (b) an internal penetration test might identify

Network policies

As well as configuration and software precautions there are procedural precautions a company can take to protect its data. Without proper procedures and policies in place, company staff may ignore or be unaware of potential threats.

An **Acceptable Use Policy** makes it clear to all network users what is acceptable and what is not.

When you started at your school you may have had to sign an Acceptable Use Policy before you were given a username and password. This policy probably said you must not use other people's accounts, access social media, play games or do anything else that is not related to your school work.

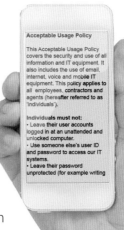

Employees will all sign a similar agreement. This is a contract between you and the school/company saying you agree to use the network only for certain things. In school you probably get away with playing games now and then but at work a company can dismiss you for going against the agreement you signed.

Preventing vulnerabilities

Anti-malware software

Anti-malware software will protect a computer in three ways:

- It prevents harmful programs from being installed on the computer
- It prevents important files, such as the operating system, from being changed or deleted
- If a virus does manage to install itself, the software will detect it when it performs regular scans. Any virus detected will be removed.

New viruses are created regularly so it is important that any antivirus software gets regular updates from the Internet.

Firewall

A computer connected to the Internet is potentially accessible to anyone else on the Internet. If a local area network, such as a school network, is connected to the Internet then all the file servers, the email server, the web server and all computers on the network are potentially accessible. Some people hack "just because they can" but often it is for identity theft or, for example, to get your bank account details so they can empty your account. Occasionally people hack with malicious intent to disrupt or destroy files or entire computer systems but this is less common.

A **firewall** is designed to prevent unauthorised access to or from a private network or intranet. All messages entering or leaving the intranet pass through the firewall, which examines each message and blocks those which do not meet specified security criteria.

Criteria may include for example:

- Where the access is from (the computer's address)
- The type of traffic (e.g. .exe files which may carry viruses)
- Specific web site addresses

A firewall doesn't just stop unwanted access from the outside world via the Internet; it can also stop computers on a network from accessing specific sites or categories of site on the network. This feature is used to stop staff in companies watching the cricket while they should be working, or from using social networking sites during working hours. In school you'll find that many sites have been blocked. Try going to a games website or getting to Facebook on a school computer and you will probably get a message saying that the site has been blocked. It is the firewall software acting as a proxy server that stops this traffic getting out of the local area network and onto the Internet.

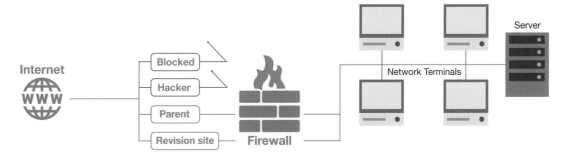

Operating systems like MS Windows have firewall utilities included but you can also buy firewall software separately. Free firewall software can also be downloaded from the Internet and many banks provide free firewall software to customers using their Internet banking services.

Password Protection

In a networked environment such as a school or a company, many of the computers are used by more than one person. Even if employees have their own computer it may be in an open plan office. The easiest way to stop unauthorised access to your computer or your files is to use a combination of a username and password.

User name:		Password		Sign in

The password should never be shared with friends or stuck on a Post-it® note under the keyboard (yes, people really do!). Also, the password should be "strong". This means that it is not easy to guess, it probably contains random letters, numbers and symbols and is at least six characters long. Some companies make employees change their password every month but this doesn't really work because people can just add the month number on the end because it is easy to remember.

For additional security against people trying lots of different passwords to get into someone else's account, the account can be locked after a certain number of failed attempts.

- using validation techniques as well as verification; when the user inputs a Username and a Password, for example checking format and field length
- setting **access levels** to minimise the risk just in case the database security has been compromised

User access levels

User access levels should be set for disks, folders and files so users can only access what they need to. At school you can probably read files on a shared area but not edit them; this is Read-Only access. The teacher will have Read-Write access to these folders. Some folders you won't even be able to see.

In a work environment, the Accounts staff will have access to payroll details but other departments will not. The Data Protection Act says that employers must keep personal data secure so setting appropriate access rights is a legal responsibility as well as a good idea.

Encryption

There are devices that can read network transmissions from the cables just by scanning the emissions; they don't even have to be plugged into the network. Also anything transmitted over a network can be intercepted and read. This takes place without leaving any trace so nobody would know that it had happened.

One way of stopping this unauthorised access to data is to encrypt anything sent on a network. Encryption changes the data before it is transmitted so it can only be deciphered by someone with the appropriate key. To anyone intercepting the message it would be unintelligible.

When you buy something on the Internet or use Internet banking you may have noticed that instead of HTTP in front of the domain name it changes to HTTPS. It works in the same way as HTTP but is encrypted so your payment details are kept secure.

3.3 – Operating systems software

The operating system is a group of programs that manages the computer's resources. These include the following functions:

- Providing a user interface
- Memory management
- Peripheral management
- User management
- File management

Providing a user interface

The user interface is the way in which we interact with computer hardware. We are all familiar with the way a PC works: clicking icons with the mouse, scrolling up and down pages, typing into forms, etc. This is called a WIMP user interface. **WIMP** stands for Windows, Icons, Menus and Pointers.

Mobile phones and tablet PCs have a slightly different user interface which allows you to move things by swiping the screen with your fingers and which can sense when you change the orientation of the device. Phones have controls that perform specific functions such as recording sound or taking a photograph.

Some computer systems are embedded in everyday machines such as cars and central heating controls. Users interact with these in different ways and the operating systems have to provide appropriate user interfaces.

Some computers have a **command-line interface**; no mouse or menus, just a text prompt where the user types a command. Before Windows came along with its **graphical user interface** (GUI) in the 1980s, PCs used this type of interface. Advanced computer users sometimes prefer a simple and direct means of controlling a program or operating system and MS Windows still provides access to a command line interface.

Whatever method is used for the user to communicate with a computer or computerised device, it is the operating system that provides these features.

Memory management

When a program is running it must be in the computer's main memory, and the operating system must manage where in memory each program and the data it needs will go. Most computers are capable of holding several programs in memory at the same time, so that a user can switch from one application to another.

When you start up a program (say, a Python program or any application software such as Word or Excel), the memory manager allocates it adequate blocks of free space in main memory. It also allocates memory for any data file that you open such as the essay you are working on in Word.

When the program finishes or no longer needs the data in previously allocated memory blocks, the memory management system frees up that space for reuse.

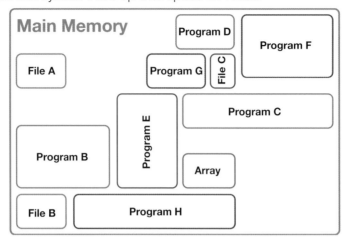

Peripheral management

Peripherals are any computer hardware components that are not part of the CPU. This includes input, output and storage devices. For some of these, the term peripheral makes sense; the keyboard and monitor, for example, are outside the main computer casing, but storage is not so obvious. Although a hard disk is usually inside the computer casing, it is still considered a peripheral as it is outside the CPU (processor and main memory). Storage devices such as portable hard disks, memory sticks and CDs are also peripherals.

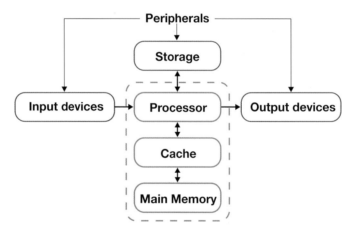

A function of the operating system is to manage these devices. When a user gives an instruction to print, the peripheral management function takes over and controls the sending of the data to be printed from memory to the device driver. (Each input or output device has its own driver – a small program that acts as an interface between the computer and the device. An HP printer, for example, will have different device drivers for a PC and a Mac, and the correct driver has to be installed so that the computer can communicate with the printer.) Meanwhile, the user can carry on editing their document in Word or whatever they were doing.

User management

User management enables a network administrator to set different access rights for different users. The software can also identify all the users currently on the network, manually log out users and monitor when and for how long each user is logged in over a period of time.

The user management system allows the administrator to set default logout times based on inactivity.

Q7 Why might a network manager want to know when and for how long each user is logged in over a period of time?

File management

A file system is normally organised into folders and subfolders for easy user navigation and usage. These folders contain files which could be software programs, databases, documents and many other types of file.

File management systems:

- enable a user to create, modify, copy, delete and move files
- enable a user to search for a particular file
- keep track of location of files on disk or other storage device so that they can be retrieved when needed
- keep track of the free space on disk where files can be stored
- enable users to restore deleted files
- prevent conflicts when two users on a network attempt to modify the same file
- maintain access rights to files

 Q8 Describe in detail **four** of the functions of a typical operating system. Explain why certain household devices may not need to have an operating system.

3.4 – Utility software

Strictly speaking the operating system is the software that controls and manages the computer system but most operating systems also include programs called utilities. Utilities are not essential for the computer to work but either make it easier for the user to use in some way, or provide housekeeping functionality. These utilities include:

- Security utilities that keep your data safe e.g. encryption software
- Disk organisation utilities that organise your files into folders and tidy up the disk
- Data compression utilities
- File backup utilities

Encryption software

Encryption tools can help to keep sensitive data safe from cyber-criminals or unauthorised access. It can also protect backup copies of data kept on offline storage. Copies of sensitive information stored on flash memory sticks or laptops and removed from the office could be vulnerable to carelessness or theft. Encrypting the data will make sure it does not fall into the wrong hands.

The encryption process uses an algorithm and a key to transform **plaintext** into **ciphertext**. To decode the original information (the plaintext), it would be necessary to know both the algorithm and the key.

Maintenance utilities

Disk defragmentation

The file management utility in Windows makes the secondary storage look like a nicely organised filing cabinet but it doesn't really look like this. Files are stored on the hard disk in blocks wherever there is space. If you have a big file it might get split up into segments so it can be stored in the available gaps. This isn't very efficient because the operating system then has to keep track of where all the segments are. After a while, thousands of files are stored in segments all over the disk. Files have become 'fragmented'.

The **disk defragmenter** moves the separate parts of the files around so that they can be stored together, which makes them quicker to access. The defragmenter also groups all the free disk space together so that new files can be stored in one place. This optimises disk performance.

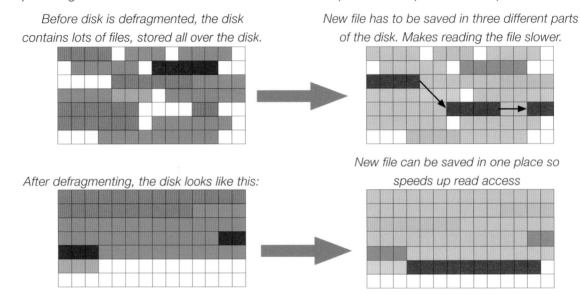

Before disk is defragmented, the disk contains lots of files, stored all over the disk.

New file has to be saved in three different parts of the disk. Makes reading the file slower.

After defragmenting, the disk looks like this:

New file can be saved in one place so speeds up read access

Automatic updating

The automatic update utility makes sure that any software installed on the computer is up-to-date. For any software already installed on the computer, the automatic update utility will regularly check the Internet for updates. These will be downloaded and installed if they are newer than the version already on the computer.

Firewalls and antivirus software must be updated regularly as new viruses and threats are constantly being devised and discovered.

Application software should also be updated as there will be bug fixes and improvements that become available to people with a licence for that package.

Compression software

Compression software such as WinZip will reduce the size of a file. There are two types of compression known as lossy and lossless; lossy compression can be used on photos where some detail is lost but this will be undetectable when viewed on screen. Lossless compression is used on text files, where it has to be possible to restore the file exactly.

Zipped or compressed files can be transmitted much more quickly over the Internet. Sometimes there is a limit to the size of a file which can be transmitted – if you have a 15MB photograph, you will not be able to email it to a friend if there is a 10MB limit on the attachments they can receive. Even if they can receive the file, it may take several minutes to download if they do not have a broadband connection.

The role and methods of backup

The staff that manage a network will back up the servers regularly. A backup is a copy of all the users' files, which can be restored in the event of files getting corrupted or deleted. Backup copies must be made regularly; how often will depend on the nature of the system.

In some organisations, a daily backup may be sufficient but in others, such as in the banking or retail industries, every transaction must be duplicated to a second and even a third storage device in a remote location.

In the case of a daily backup, copies are normally made to a removable hard disk or cassette tape. The medium has to be high capacity and portable so it can be stored in a fire-proof safe or off site.

When you work on a project at school and save it in your user area on the school network, you are probably completely confident that it will still be available even if there is a catastrophic event like a hard disk crash. One method of ensuring that backups are safe is to save them in Cloud storage. The provider will have several huge data warehouses and will have copies of all data stored held at multiple sites.

Full backup and incremental backup

It is not always necessary to make up a full backup of all files on a system. A more efficient method is to do an incremental backup, in which only new files or files which have changed since the last backup, are copied to the backup file. Software files, for example, are unlikely to change very often. Many data files will only be changed occasionally.

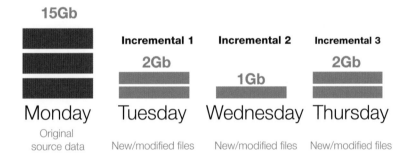

Restoring form a backup

If a disaster occurs and the system has to be restored from the backup, it is much quicker to restore from a full backup. The entire contents can simply be copied onto a new hard drive.

When restoring from incremental back-up, it is necessary to have the most recent full back-up files as well as every incremental back-up that has been made since the last full back-up.

For example, a full back-up was made on Monday and incremental back-ups were made on Tuesday, Wednesday and Thursday. If it is necessary to restore the back-up on Friday morning, it would require all four back-up files: Monday's full backup plus the incremental backup for Tuesday, Wednesday and Thursday.

Archiving

Often there is a large amount of data stored on a computer system that is no longer needed on a regular basis. However, you cannot delete it, in case it is needed again or because a company is legally required to keep some records for a number of years (for example tax returns). The data can be taken off the main system and archived, stored usually on magnetic tape as it is cheap. It can be loaded back onto the system if it is needed again. The purpose is to free up space on the main computer system.

Exercises

1. (a)   What is "phishing"?   [2]

    (b)   Describe **two** ways that it is often possible to detect a phishing email.   [2]

    (c)   Explain what is meant by a "Denial of Service" (DOS) attack.   [2]

    (d)   Describe **one** way that a criminal may use to perpetrate a DOS attack.   [1]

2. A school has all of its computers in a local area network (LAN).

    (a)   State **two** benefits of a LAN.   [2]

    (b)   Explain **two** measures which the school will need to take to ensure the security
          of the network.   [4]

    OCR A451 Jan 2013 Qu 5

3. State which **four** of the tasks listed below are carried out by the operating system.   [4]

    (a)   Carrying out a spellcheck

    (b)   Managing emails

    (c)   Creating new folders on a storage device

    (d)   Setting tab spaces

    (e)   Multitasking

    (f)   Organising hardware resources

    (g)   Managing virtual storage

    (h)   Sorting a database

4. Harry complains that reading data from his disk has become very slow.

    (a)   Explain **two** possible reasons for this.   [2]

    (b)   Explain what action he should case in each of these cases.   [2]

5   (a)   Explain the difference between backup and archiving.   [2]

    (b)   Explain what is meant by an incremental backup and how this would be carried out.   [2]

6. Julia buys a new laptop with a system information utility and a diagnosis utility. Give an
    example of each and describe its purpose.

          System information utility: [1]
          Example: [1]
          Diagnosis utility: [1]
          Example: [1]

    OCR A451/01 June 2014 Qu 8

Section 4

Ethical, legal, cultural and environmental concerns

Objectives

- Investigate the following issues related to Computer Science technologies:

  o   ethical issues

  o   legal issues

  o   cultural issues

  o   environmental issues

  o   privacy issues

- Understand how key stakeholders are affected by technologies

- Consider the environmental impact of Computer Science

- Consider the cultural implications of Computer Science

- Compare open source with proprietary software

- Study legislation relevant to Computer Science:

  o   The Data Protection Act 1998

  o   Computer Misuse Act 1990

  o   Copyright Designs and Patents Act 1988

  o   Creative Commons Licensing

  o   Freedom of Information Act 2000

4.1 – Computer systems in the modern world

Computer technology impacts just about everything we do. Here are a few areas to consider.

Communication

We can keep in touch with friends and family all over the world through email, texting, phone calls and social networking sites. The latest news about world events can be spread instantly. We can find out whether a train is on time, what's on at the cinema, or exactly where a friend is at this moment, using our smartphones.

Can you imagine having to wait months for news of a family member who has emigrated to another country?

Employment

Computer technology has had a huge impact on employment. Many types of work have disappeared, and new jobs have been created.

Computer technology has already led to the loss of thousands of different jobs, for example in:

- clerical work
- manufacturing
- the photographic industry

Robots could soon surpass humans in routine legal work, language translation and medical diagnosis – but plumbers, gardeners and physiotherapists will be hard to replace.

Thousands of new jobs have been created as a result of computer technology:

- software and hardware development
- creation of a multitude of new products from robots, "smart homes" and mobile technologies to online learning materials and aids for disabled people

> **Q1** Name three jobs that you think could be computerised, and five jobs that cannot easily be computerised.

Shopping

Online shopping has led to the closing of many High Street stores. It has also helped people who find it difficult to get to a supermarket for their food shopping.

Manufacturing

Computer technology is used in manufacturing to produce items faster, more accurately and cheaper than can be done by hand. Think how technology is used in the manufacture of:

- clothing
- cars
- building materials
- electronics

 Computers are involved in some way or another in almost every manufacturing industry in the UK. How have they affected other industries such as farming?

Recent developments in software

For years, computer companies have been developing software programs to take on human opponents in games such as chess. **Deep Blue** was the first chess-playing computer to beat a world champion in 1996 when it defeated Gary Kasparov, the reigning world champion.

Go is a Chinese game significantly more complex than chess, played by millions of people all over the world. It is played on a 19 x 19 grid, with one player placing black stones and the other placing white stones, the object being to control more territory than your opponent. It has long been an objective in the field of artificial intelligence (AI) to develop software to beat a human champion.

Case sudy: DeepMind AlphaGo program

In March 2016 world champion Go player Lee Se-dol from South Korea was defeated by Google's DeepMind AlphaGo program. This was the first time a computer had been able to beat a human player at the game.

The program taught itself how to improve by splitting itself in half and playing millions of matches against itself, learning from each victory and loss. In one day alone, AlphaGo was able to play itself more than a million times, gaining more experience than a human player could in a lifetime.

The co-founder Demis Hassabis said he hoped to use the same technique to help Google improve its products, such as its phone assistants and search engine. "The software learns by trial and error, incrementally improving and learning from its mistakes so that it makes better decisions."

Driverless cars

Google's driverless cars are already being tested on Britain's roads. But what of the legal issues? Will the car be able to distinguish between a fox, a child and a plastic bag and make the appropriate decision about what action to take?

If someone is hurt or killed by a driverless car, who is to blame? The manufacturer, the owner of the car, or the person in charge of the car at the time?

Q3 What are the benefits and drawbacks of driverless cars?

The rise of artificial intelligence

Where will we go next? Science fiction is full of stories of robots that plot against their human creators and ultimately replace them.

A 2016 YouGov survey for the British Science Association of more than 2,000 people found that:

- 60% think that the use of robots or programs equipped with artificial intelligence (AI) will lead to fewer jobs within ten years.

- 36% of the public believe that the development of AI poses a threat to the long term survival of humanity.

- Generally, people don't trust robots to take on roles where their lives could be in danger. Respondents would not trust robots to carry out surgical procedures (53%), drive public buses (49%) or fly commercial aircraft (62%).

- 13% of men, but only 6% of women, thought they could be friends with a robot.

- 28% of 18-24 year-olds thought that robots could be future co-workers and ten per cent imagined that they could regard them as family members.

Q4 What do you think about these issues? What are your reasons in each case? What are the cultural issues involved here?

Environmental impact of computers

Environmental issues include the carbon footprint and waste products that result from manufacturing computer systems, but this is often outweighed by the positive effects on the environment of using computerised systems to manage processes that might otherwise generate more pollution.

Considerations may include:

- Does a computer system mean that people can work from home and therefore drive less?

- Has computer technology led to a "throw-away society", with huge waste dumps of unwanted products which are thrown away rather than repaired or upgraded?

- Is working at home more environmentally friendly than everyone working in a big office, in terms of heating and lighting?
- Do computer-managed engines work more efficiently? Create less pollution and use less fuel?

Computers and waste

The pace of technology is so rapid that computers, mobile phones and handheld-devices that seemed so desirable a few short years ago are now discarded without a thought for the latest must-have piece of equipment. Are they recyclable or are they simply contributing to a huge mountain of waste, containing dangerous chemical elements which leach into water supplies in developing countries?

Computer-aided manufacturing can result in more and cheaper products. But does this lead to more waste? Disposable coffee cups used in their millions every day by people at work are cheap to make, thanks to modern technology. They are made from paper laminated with plastic, and so are largely unrecyclable. Three billion coffee cups were handed out last year in coffee shops in the UK, and fewer than one in 400 was recycled.

Q5 Think of some other ways in which computers have helped to decrease environmental pollution, by monitoring the environment or by replacing old polluting industries with more environmentally friendly products, for example in the energy industry.

Computers and safety

Many dangerous jobs can now be done by remote controlled devices and sensors. For example:

- bomb disposal robots can destroy bombs remotely
- devices can sense poisonous gases in mines
- weather data can be collected from the top of a mountain or from inside a volcano without a scientist having to go into these dangerous situations every day to collect it

Using data collected about weather, volcanic activity, and movement beneath the earth's surface, people can be warned about impending disasters such as hurricanes and earthquakes, and moved to safety.

4.2 – Ethical and cultural issues

Computers have become so widespread that we cannot imagine life without them. What impact has this had on our culture? For example:

- Have we become a more, or a less caring society?
- Do we work less hard now that computers are able to do so many jobs formerly done by humans, or are we in fact working harder than ever?
- Has it become more acceptable to be rude to or bully complete strangers now that this is possible online?
- Are women more equal now that housework and cooking occupy a small fraction of the time that they used to?

Q6 Think of some other ways in which computer technology has changed the way we live and work.

Key stakeholders in technology

A **stakeholder** is anyone who is affected by the actions, objectives or policies of an organisation such as the government, company or school. A **key stakeholder** could be the owner of a company, a supplier or the community affected by the decisions and policies of an organisation.

We are all affected to a greater or lesser extent by developments in technology.

Computers in healthcare

Computers plays a hugely important role in healthcare. As well as the administrative tasks that computers perform, they are used for example to monitor patients, administer drugs, and diagnose illnesses. There are now more than 165,000 health-related apps which run on one or other of the two main smart-phone operating systems, Apple's iOS and Google's Android.

These apps will have been downloaded 1.7 billion times by 2017. Check out, for example, **your.MD** online to see how one of these apps works.

As these apps become more popular, there are concerns that some health apps may be sharing patients' health data without their knowledge.

 Q7 What sort of data might be shared? Who would it be shared with, and how could this impact an individual?

Computer-aided diagnosis is being used to improve diagnosis and treatment.

These tools need to be scrutinised ethically as well as scientifically or economically; would we be happy with a diagnostic tool that saved lives overall but discriminated against some patients? Who is responsible for computer-based decisions in healthcare?

 Q8 It has been suggested that computers could replace human beings in healthcare decision-making. Discuss the cultural and ethical issues involved in such a scenario.

Social networking

Many people of all ages use social networking sites and Twitter to keep in touch with friends and family. If you are out and about, you are more likely to post a photograph and a comment on Facebook than send a postcard. You can communicate with friends and family all over world very easily.

As well as keeping in touch, people use internet dating sites to meet people rather than going to bars and clubs. Social networking using computer technology has become normal. Some people think this is great because you can have more "friends" but others think we are losing the ability to socially interact face-to-face.

Digital exposure carries risks. A recent survey by Parent Zone revealed that although 74.5% of teenagers report that the Internet made them happy, 36% admitted they would suggest friends avoid Facebook if they were feeling worried or upset.

 Q9 What are the dangers of social networking sites such as Facebook? What are the benefits?

The rating culture

Using a mobile phone, you can keep in constant touch with all your friends. You can make new "friends", and find out a lot about them. You can use your phone to find your way around, check out the look of a place you are going to visit, book a cinema ticket, a holiday or a taxi ride.

You can then rate people, places and events, giving them a score based on what you thought of them. Let's look more closely at this practice.

On the face of it, being able to look at the average rating of a film, book, restaurant or holiday destination seems a very helpful idea. But it can go further than that.

Case study: Rating taxi drivers

When you book a taxi through Uber, for example, you can rate the driver. Passengers are essentially unpaid supervisors of the company, monitoring drivers' behaviour so that Uber can manage its workforce. The passengers have quite a lot of power here – if an Uber driver's score dips below 4.6 out of 5 they may get "deactivated" and no longer drive for Uber. But a lot of people might consider that 4.6 out of 5 is a very good score.

So what is a driver being scored on? Type of car is a big factor. Uber suggests that drivers should offer water to the passengers. Really? If the driver can't find that little pub in a back street of a big city where you're meeting your friends, do you give him or her a bad score?

And don't forget, as a passenger, the driver can rate you, too.

Q10 What factors would you take into consideration when rating an Uber taxi driver?

Rating goes far beyond Uber. There are apps that let you rate your co-workers, your teachers, pupils and bosses. The Peeple app launched in March 2016 lets you rate other people, "Revolutionising the way we're seen in the world, through our relationships." You can rate anyone you come in contact with in three ways – personally, professionally and romantically – provided you allow yourself to be "recommended" by others.

Q11 Does this get you better job opportunities, better dates, better networking opportunities? What are the upsides, downsides and dangers of using a site like this? Can humans be rated?

 Q12 Do some research on the Internet and find out more about these two applications.

Risks of digital technology

- In-car satellite-navigation systems are commonly programmed to find the quickest route to your destination. Is it ethical to program a route to a popular destination which takes a multitude of drivers through a previously quiet, safe residential neighbourhood where there may be children playing outside?

- There is an obvious danger posed by the fact that a simple 3D print file can be downloaded from the Internet and a gun fabricated within hours. Should there be a blanket ban on sharing such files? Is it even possible to impose such a ban?

4.3 – Legislation and privacy

Legal issues

The law can affect the way that computer systems are developed, how they are used and how they are disposed of, for example.

The Data Protection Act 1998

The Data Protection Act says that anyone who stores personal details must keep them secure. Companies with computer systems that store any personal data must have processes and security mechanisms designed into the system to meet this requirement.

The act includes a number of principles:

- data must be processed fairly and lawfully
- data must be adequate, relevant and not excessive
- data must be accurate and up to date
- data must not be retained for longer than necessary

- data can only be used for the purpose for which it was collected
- data must be kept secure
- data must be handled in accordance with people's rights
- data must not be transferred outside the EU without adequate protection.

> **Q13** An accountant's practice were found to have thrown old customer records from 2005 in the waste bins outside their offices. Which principle(s) of the Act may have been broken?

The Freedom of Information Act 2000

In 2000, a new law was passed to give people access to data held by public authorities, including state schools, police forces, local authorities and the NHS. It does not give access to personal data about people, but it means, for example, that anyone can ask for a list of all the state schools in a certain area.

The Computer Misuse Act 1990

The Computer Misuse Act has three main principles, primarily designed to prevent unauthorised access or 'hacking' of programs or data.

The Computer Misuse Act (1990) recognised the following new offences:

- Unauthorised access to computer material
- Unauthorised access with intent to commit or facilitate a crime
- Unauthorised modification of computer material

> **Q14** Describe some behaviours which would be illegal under this Act

The Copyright Designs and Patents Act 1988

This Act is designed to protect the creators of books, music, video and software from having their work illegally copied.

The Act makes it illegal to use, copy or distribute commercially available software without buying the appropriate licence. When a computer system is designed and implemented, licensing must be considered in terms of which software should be used.

If you buy a music CD or pay to download a piece of music, software or a video, it is illegal to:

- pass a copy to a friend
- make a copy and then sell it
- use the software on a network, unless the licence allows it

The software industry can take some steps to prevent illegal copying of software:

- The user must enter a unique key before the software is installed
- Some software will only run if the CD is present in the drive
- Some applications will only run if a special piece of hardware called a 'dongle' is plugged into a USB port on the computer

Creative Commons Licensing

A **Creative Commons** licence is used when an author is willing to give people the right to share or use a work that they have created, for example a set of lesson plans or a book, play or video they have written or made. The creator can choose to allow only non-commercial use, so that their work cannot be copied and distributed for profit.

Open Source and proprietary software

As computers and mobile technology becomes cheaper and ever more widely available worldwide, more and more consideration has to be given to the type of software – free or paid for? The different categories are described below.

Open Source software is governed by the Open Source Initiative that says:

- Software is licensed for use but there is no charge for the licence. Anyone can use it.
- Open Source software must be distributed with the source code so anyone can modify it.
- Developers can sell the software they have created.
- Any new software created from Open Source software must also be 'open'. This means that it must be distributed or sold in a form that other people can read and also edit.

This is different from **Freeware** (free software) which may be free to use but the user does not get access to the source code. Freeware usually has restrictions on its use as well.

Proprietary software is sold in the form of a licence to use it.

- There will be restrictions on how the software can be used, for example the license may specify only one concurrent user, or it may permit up to a certain number of users on one site (site licence).
- The company or person who wrote the software will hold the copyright. The users will not have access to the source code and will not be allowed to modify the package and sell it to other people. This would infringe the copyright (Copyright, Designs and Patents Act).

The benefit of using proprietary software is the support available from the company. There will be regular updates available and technical support lines, training courses and a large user base. Open Source software tends to be more organic – it changes over time as developers modify source code and distribute new versions. There isn't a commercial organisation behind the software so there probably won't be a helpline or regular updates, just a community of enthusiastic developers.

Privacy issues

According to the head of a Royal Academy study into surveillance, Google is within a few years of having sufficient information to be able to track the exact movements and intentions of every individual, via Google Earth and other software they are developing.

It is predicted that small computers will become embedded in everything from clothes to beermats. Consequently, we will be interfacing with computers in everything we do, from meeting chip-wearing strangers to entering smart buildings or sitting on a smart sofa, and each of these interfaces will end up on a Google database.

It is a vision of a world without privacy.

Already, Google collects and stores data about millions of emails every day.

Organisations including governments and security agencies, collect huge amounts of data about private citizens, often supplied by Internet and telephone companies.

With the aim of detecting terrorist or other illegal activities, the US Government collects, stores and monitors metadata about electronic communications. **Metadata** includes information such as the telephone number called, date, time and duration of call.

In one month in 2013, the unit collected data on more than 97 billion emails and 124 billion phone calls from around the world. Edward Snowden is a famous 'whistle-blower' who informed the world about these practices.

> **Q15** Why do some people object to this data being collected and stored? What are the arguments for and against collecting such data?

Using cookies

Cookies are files, often including unique identifiers, that are sent by web servers to web browsers, and which may then be sent back to the server each time the browser requests a page from the server.

They are used:

- to recognise your computer when you revisit a website
- to track you as you navigate the website, and to enable the use of any e-commerce facilities
- to improve the website's usability
- to analyse the use of the website
- in the administration of the website
- to personalise the website for you, including targeted advertisements which may be of particular interest to you.

Some websites remind you that they will collect data about you:

Hacking

In May 2015, a computer security expert flying on a passenger airliner hacked into the aircraft's computer controls through the entertainment system and briefly made it fly sideways. He told the FBI he did this to demonstrate the vulnerabilities in the computer system so that they would be fixed.

Case study: Hacking into smart meters

GCHQ, the British Government intelligence and security organisation, has intervened in the design of an £11bn nationwide system of smart meters to secure them against attempts by hackers to crash the country's power grids. The agency discovered loopholes in the system that it believes could pose a national security threat by causing a collapse in the national grid system by potentially gaining control of every meter.

The meters automatically send readings back to the energy suppliers instead of the householder or an employee of the energy company having to read gas and electricity meters. The new metering system is one of the biggest IT projects in a generation. Energy companies have already installed about two million of the 53 million smart meters due to be installed across the country by 2020.

Exercises

1. Robots are being introduced into a factory which makes computer components.

    (a) Describe **three** ways in which this could affect workers. [3]

    (b) The management thinks that using robots will reduce costs. Give **three** ways in which costs may be reduced. [3]

    (c) Give **two** other advantages to management of introducing robots. [2]

2. A large online retailer, Thames Online, uses software to manage its customer accounts. The software makes decisions about customer accounts based on how many times they have ordered and how many times they have returned the goods because they arrived damaged, late or not as described.

    Over the last two years Jason has ordered 350 items from Thames Online, and has sent 36 of them back. The software marks his account as "blocked" and Jason cannot order any more goods. He also cannot use the £100 Thames Online gift voucher that his aunt sent him for his birthday. He also cannot claim a refund for the his "Five Star Service" subscription of £70 per annum, which guarantees next day delivery on all goods, even though he is only two months into the year.

    Discuss the ethical issues involved in this scenario. [6]

3. A school uses off the shelf, proprietary software for managing pupils' attendance, and customised, open source software for managing pupils' examinations.

    (a) Describe the difference between off the shelf and custom written software. [2]

    (b) Describe the difference between proprietary and open source software. [2]

    (c) Explain the legal issues that the school should consider when choosing the software for managing pupils' attendance and examinations.

    The quality of written communication will be assessed in your answer to this question [6]

    OCR A451 June 2013 Qu 9

4. The organiser of a charity Fun Run stores personal information about the participants. The Data Protection Act gives participants the right to know what data is stored about them. Two principles of the Data Protection Act are:

    • data must be processed fairly and lawfully

    • data must be adequate, relevant and not excessive

    State **three** other principles of the Act. [3]

5. Some governments and security services may collect data about all telephone calls and email communications made by their citizens. This may amount to several billion records every month. They argue that they cannot keep their citizens safe from terrorism unless they have access to private data.

    Give arguments in support of and against this practice. [5]

Section 5

Algorithms

Objectives

- Understand and apply computational thinking methods including abstraction, decomposition and algorithmic thinking

- Understand and trace linear and binary searching algorithms

- Describe and trace bubble, insertion and merge sort algorithms

- Learn how to produce algorithms using flow diagrams and pseudocode

- Interpret, correct or complete algorithms

5

5.1 – Computational thinking

Computer Science is all about studying problems and figuring out how to solve them. The problem might be a mathematical one like adding the numbers 1 to 100, or finding all the prime numbers less than a million. Or, it might be something less well-defined, like getting a computer to recognise when the platform of an underground railway is becoming dangerously full. It could be a problem that a virus-checker attempts to solve – detecting when your computer has a virus.

A human being looking at a CCTV of an Underground platform would be able to tell quite easily if it was too crowded, and no more people should be allowed through the barrier. But how do we get a computer to recognise that situation?

Some of the key concepts in computational thinking include:

- abstraction
- decomposition
- algorithmic thinking

Abstraction

Abstraction involves removing unnecessary details from a problem in order to solve it. We are all familiar with the idea of abstracting away details from abstract paintings and statues; think of the famous statue "Angel of the North" by Anthony Gormley, dominating the skyline near the A1 at Gateshead.

How can this principle be applied to the problem of recognising a crowded platform? The computer needs to pick out the relevant objects and ignore the rest. It can ignore the background lights, the colour of the clothes people are wearing, whether they are carrying rucksacks and whether they are male or female. The only important fact is how many heads can be detected.

> **Q1** Can you think of any other way a computer could figure out whether a platform is overcrowded? Is the presence of the train relevant?

Abstraction is used in thousands of different ways to aid in problem-solving. One common method of problem-solving is by using simulation – building a model of a problem and finding out what happens under different circumstances. Of course, it does not have to be a physical model; it is more likely to be what is termed a "logical" model, that is, one which describes the basic facts and does a lot of calculations to help predict what will happen in different circumstances. Simulations of this sort include:

- climate change models

- financial models like a "lemonade stand model" to calculate whether your lemonade stand is likely to make a profit

- population models to help predict the likely population in 20 years' time, based on current trends

- queueing models, to help estimate how many toll-booths will be needed on a new motorway, or how many checkouts there need to be in a new supermarket

 What would be the inputs to each of these models? How is abstraction used in each case?

Abstraction allows us to separate the "logical" from the "physical". A good example of this is the map of the London Underground – all we need to know is what stations are on which line, and the best route to get from A to B. There is no need to get bogged down in details of the exact distance between stations or even in which direction the route actually takes us at any given moment.

Similarly, we are all quite happy to use a computer or drive a car without having much idea of how it works. A driver, a child in the back seat and a mechanic all have very different views of a car. We abstract away everything we don't need to know about and concentrate on the essentials.

5

Decomposition

Decomposition involves the breaking down of a problem into smaller, simpler steps or stages. For example, imagine we are writing a computer game which has many complex levels. We could break it up as follows:

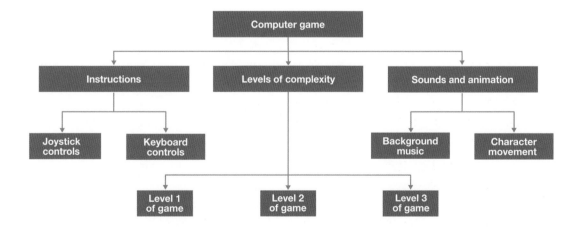

Each of the boxes could be further sub-divided until each box represents a single, simple sub-task. When tasks are broken down in this way, i.e. **decomposed**, it becomes much easier to solve the problem. Each small part of it is itself a small, manageable subproblem for which the steps in a solution can be written down.

Algorithmic thinking

When you started programming, your whole program fitted on the screen. It was really easy to see what was going on and fix the problems. As programs get much bigger they become unmanageable so we need to break them into smaller sections.

Also, when we start with a user problem in real life, the problem is going to be much more complex than the ones we're looking at on a GCSE course. Writing the code is the easy part; working out exactly what the code has to do is more difficult. The series of steps the program has to perform to solve the problem is called an **algorithm**.

A working algorithm will always finish and return an answer or perform the task it was supposed to. "Always finishes" is something you may take for granted until you write a program that gets stuck in an infinite loop (always save before you run your program!).

Let's take a step back from programming for a moment. Other sorts of algorithm that you may be familiar with are: recipes, direction, knitting patterns, instruction for flat-pack furniture.

Here's a problem:

How do I get from Trafalgar Square to Buckingham Palace?

An algorithm does not have to be written in code. The first steps to working out the design will be to draw diagrams and/or list the steps involved.

We will be looking at how to break down the problem and then structure a solution using some standard tools called **flow diagrams** and **pseudocode**.

Only when the solution has some structure can you effectively start coding it. Pseudocode is the first step to actual code as it outlines the algorithm in programming constructs but doesn't rely on any specific language syntax.

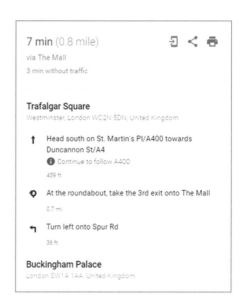

7 min (0.8 mile)

via The Mall
3 min without traffic

Trafalgar Square
Westminster, London WC2N 5DN, United Kingdom

↑ Head south on St. Martin's Pl/A400 towards Duncannon St/A4
ⓘ Continue to follow A400
459 ft

◉ At the roundabout, take the 3rd exit onto The Mall
0.7 mi

↰ Turn left onto Spur Rd
36 ft

Buckingham Palace
London SW1A 1AA, United Kingdom

Q3 Here is an algorithm.

```
x = 0
repeat 10 times
    ask user to enter a mark
    accept the mark
    if mark > x then x = mark
endrepeat
print x
```

What does this algorithm print if the numbers 14, 7, 16, 12, 10, 8, 12, 9, 11, 8 are entered?

What would make this algorithm easier to understand?

Q4 Write an algorithm to add up the numbers from 1 to 100.

5.2 – Searching algorithms

Before starting to write algorithms for our problems, we will look at some well-known algorithms for searching and sorting, which are both very common operations in the real world.

Thousands of software applications, such as databases or commercial search engines such as Google, depend on the ability to search through huge amounts of data to find a particular item.

> **Q5** Name some other organisations that store huge amounts of data which often need to be searched to quickly find a particular item.

We are going to consider two search algorithms in this section:

* Linear search
* Binary search

A linear search

When the data is unsorted, the only sensible option when searching for a particular item is to start at the beginning and look at every item until you find the one you want. You could be lucky and find the item quite quickly if it's near the beginning of the list, or you could be unlucky and find it right at the end of the list.

> **Q6** If you have a list of 10,000 unsorted names, on average how many items will need to be examined until you find the one you are looking for?

> **Q7** How many items will you look at if the item is not in the list?

Here is an algorithm for a linear search:

```
1.    found = False
2.    Start at the first name
3.  do
4.      Examine the current name in the list
5.      if it's the one you are looking for then found = True
6.  until found = True OR reach end of list
7.  if found = True then
8.      print (name)
9.  else
10.     print ("Not found")
11. endif
```

The algorithm as written is a long way from something you can turn into program code, but it describes how you might go about solving the problem.

Example 1

Look at the following list of integers:

14	2	3	11	1	9	5	8	10	6

The items you would examine to find the number **5** would be: **14, 2, 3, 11, 1, 9, 5**

Q8 Write down the items you would examine to locate data item **11** in the above data list.

A binary search

If the list is sorted, (i.e. in numerical or alphabetical order), you can use a much more efficient algorithm called a binary search. It works by repeatedly dividing in half the portion of the data list that could contain the required data item. This is continued until there is only one item in the list.

This is the algorithm:

```
1.    found = False
2.    while there are more items in the list AND found == False
3.        Examine the middle data item in the list
4.        if this is the required item, then
5.            found = True
5.        else
6.            if required item > middle item then
7.                discard the first half of the list
8.            else
9.                discard the second half of the list
10.           endif
11.       endif
12.   endwhile
```

Example 2

Consider the following ordered list where we wish to search for data item **50.**

15	21	29	32	37	40	42	43	48	50	60	64	77	81	90

Stage 1: middle term is **43**; we can therefore discard all data items less than or equal to 64.

48	50	60	64	77	81	90

Stage 2: middle term is **64**, so we can discard all data items greater than or equal to 64

48	50	60

Stage 3: middle term is **50** – so we have found the data item.

Notice that if there are an even number of items in the list, for example 8 items, the fourth, not the fifth, item is taken to be the middle item.

Q9 Suppose we have the following sorted list of 10 items:

3	5	6	8	11	12	14	15	17	18

Which one of the following is the correct sequence of comparisons when used to locate the data item **8**?

(i)   12, 6, 8   (iii)   3, 5, 6, 8

(ii)   11, 5, 6, 8   (iv)   11, 6, 5, 8

Q10 Ask a friend to think of a number between 1 and 1000. Then use a binary search algorithm to guess the number. How many different guesses will you need, at most?

Q11 Look at the following data list. Which items will you examine in (a) a linear search and (b) a binary search to find the following data items:

    (i)   27

    (ii) 11

    (iii) 60

9	11	19	22	27	30	32	33	40	42	50	54	57	61	70	78	85

5.3 – Sorting algorithms

In the last sub-section we looked at methods of searching for data. The binary search method required the data to be sorted before the search could take place. There are many algorithms for sorting data and we will look at three of them:

* Bubble sort
* Insertion sort
* Merge sort

Bubble sort

A bubble sort works by repeatedly going through the list to be sorted, comparing each pair of adjacent elements. If the elements are in the wrong order they are swapped. A short algorithm to do the swapping is:

```
temp = a
a = b
b = temp
```

If `a = 9` and `b = 6`, the **trace table** below shows that the values of a and b have been swapped.

temp	a	b
	9	6
9	6	9

Q12 Why could we not just write the two statements below to swap the values?

```
a = b
b = a
```

Example 3: Working through the Bubble sort algorithm

The figure below shows how the items change order in the first pass, as the largest item 'bubbles' to the end of the list. Each time an item is larger than the next one, they change places.

Pass 1

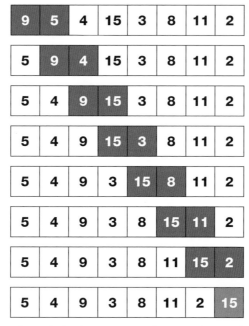

After the first pass, the largest item is in the correct place at the end of the list. On the second pass, only the first seven numbers are checked.

End of Pass 2

11 and 15 are in the correct place; so only the first six numbers are checked.

End of Pass 3

9, 11 and 15 are in the correct place; so only the first five numbers are checked.

End of Pass 4

8, 9, 11 and 15 are in the correct place; so only the first four numbers are checked.

End of Pass 5

5, 8, 9, 11 and 15 are in the correct place; so only the first three numbers are checked.

End of Pass 6

Finally, the first two numbers are checked and swapped.

Pass 7

```
numbers = [9, 5, 4, 15, 3, 8, 11, 2]
numItems = len(numbers)   //get number of items in the array
for i = 0 to numItems - 2
  for j = 0 to numItems - i - 2
    if numbers[j] > numbers[j + 1] then
        temp = numbers[j]
        numbers[j] = numbers[j + 1]
        numbers[j + 1] = temp
    endif
  next j
  print (numbers)
next i
```

If you run this program, the output is:

```
[5, 4, 9, 3, 8, 11, 2, 15]
[4, 5, 3, 8, 9, 2, 11, 15]
[4, 3, 5, 8, 2, 9, 11, 15]
[3, 4, 5, 2, 8, 9, 11, 15]
[3, 4, 2, 5, 8, 9, 11, 15]
[3, 2, 4, 5, 8, 9, 11, 15]
[2, 3, 4, 5, 8, 9, 11, 15]
```

Q13 Carry out a bubble sort on the following set of numbers. The numbers are to be sorted in ASCENDING ORDER (lowest to highest).

6	8	1	17	27	11	15	3	14	42	5

(a) What is the order of the items after the first pass?

(b) How many passes through the data will be made?

What is the maximum number of passes on a list of 2 items?

What is the maximum number of passes on a list of 3 items? 10,000 items?

Insertion sort

This is a sorting algorithm that sorts one data item at a time. It is rather similar to how you might sort a hand of cards. The algorithm takes one data item from the list and places it in the correct location in the list. This process is repeated until there are no more unsorted data items in the list. Although more efficient that the bubble sort, it is not as efficient as the merge sort or quick sort.

Example 4: Insertion sort

The same list of numbers is sorted into ascending order using an insertion sort:

9, 5, 4, 15, 3, 8, 11, 2

We leave the first item at the start of the list			9	5	4	15	3	8	11	2

We leave the first item at the start of the list — **9** 5 4 15 3 8 11 2

5 is now inserted into the sorted list — **1st pass** — **5 9** 4 15 3 8 11 2

4 is now inserted into the sorted list — **2nd pass** — **4 5 9** 15 3 8 11 2

15 is now inserted into the sorted list (it stays where it is) — **3rd pass** — **4 5 9 15** 3 8 11 2

3 is now inserted into the sorted list — **4th pass** — **3 4 5 9 15** 8 11 2

8 is now inserted into the sorted list — **5th pass** — **3 4 5 8 9 15** 11 2

11 is now inserted into the sorted list — **6th pass** — **3 4 5 8 9 11 15** 2

2 is now inserted into the sorted list — **7th pass** — **2 3 4 5 8 9 11 15**

On each pass, the current data item is checked against those already in the sorted list (shown in grey in the diagram). If the data item being compared in the sorted list is larger than the current data item, it is shifted to the right. This continues until we reach a data item in the sorted list which is smaller than the current data item.

For example, at the 5th pass 8 is compared with 15, and since 8 is smaller, 15 is shifted right.

8 is compared with 9, and 9 is shifted right.

8 is compared with 5, and as 8 is larger, it is inserted into the free space.

5th pass in summary:

8 is removed from the list temporarily — **3 4 5 9 15** _ 11 2

Since 15 > 8, it is now shifted to the right — **3 4 5 9** _ 15 11 2

Since 9 > 8, it is now shifted to the right — **3 4 5** _ 9 15 11 2

Since 5 < 8, 8 is now inserted into the sorted list — **3 4 5 8 9 15** 40 53

> **Q14** The following list of names is to be sorted into alphabetical sequence using an insertion sort. George, Jane, Miranda, Ahmed, Sophie, Bernie, Keith.
>
> (a) What is the first name to be moved? What will the list look like after this name is moved?
>
> (b) What is the second name to be moved? What will the list look like after this name has been moved?
>
> (c) How many names have to be moved altogether before the list is sorted?

Merge sort

This is a two stage sort. In the first stage, the list is successively divided in half, forming two sublists, until each sublist is of length one.

Example 5: Sorting in ascending order

Stage 1

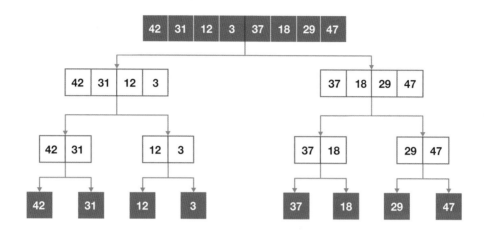

This is the end of stage 1 where all the elements have been separated out.

In the second stage, each pair of sublists is repeatedly merged to produce new sorted sublists until there is only one sublist remaining. This is the sorted list.

Stage 2

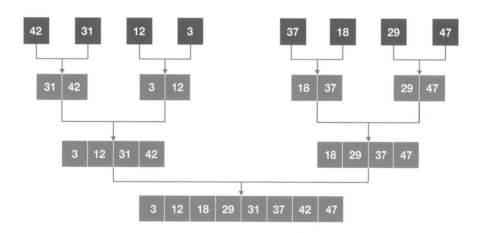

This is the end of stage 2, with all the items recombined in sorted order.

Q15 Carry out a merge sort on the following set of numbers. The numbers are to be sorted in ascending order.

| 6 | 8 | 1 | 17 | 27 | 11 | 15 | 3 |

(a) Write out the 4 sublists after the first stage of the merge process.

(b) Write out the next 2 sublists of the merge process.

(c) Write out the complete list after the second stage of the merge process.

(d) Which algorithm, the bubble or the merge sort, do you think is more efficient?

5.4 – Developing algorithms using flow diagrams

In computing we write programs or create computer systems to "solve a problem". The **problem** is the need or requirement we have to meet. The solution could be a simple program but is more likely to be a complex suite of hardware and software in a real-world scenario, which will need to be broken down into many programs and subroutines.

Understanding how to solve the problem is important. You cannot just start coding at line 1 and hope to get a working solution straight away. The first step is to write an **algorithm** – that is, the series of steps needed to solve the problem.

This section will consider how algorithms are developed with the aid of **flow diagrams** and **pseudocode**. Flow diagrams are diagrams which use certain symbols to show the flow of data, processing and input/output taking place in a program or task.

Standard flow diagram symbols

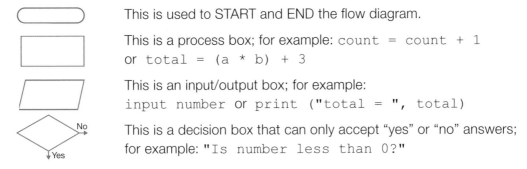

This is used to START and END the flow diagram.

This is a process box; for example: `count = count + 1` or `total = (a * b) + 3`

This is an input/output box; for example: `input number` or `print ("total = ", total)`

This is a decision box that can only accept "yes" or "no" answers; for example: `"Is number less than 0?"`

Example 6

In this flow diagram, the value called `number` is continuously multiplied by 2 and the value is added to `sum` after each iteration of the loop. The loop continues until the value of `sum` exceeds 29; at this point, `sum` is output.

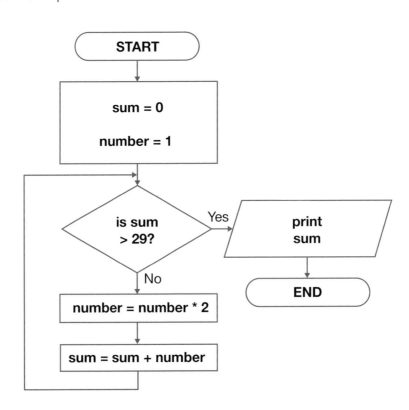

Q16 Complete the trace table to show how `sum` and `number` increase. What is output by the algorithm?

number	sum	sum > 29?
1	0	No

Q17 The following flow diagram inputs 365 temperatures and outputs the number of days when the temperature was more than 20°C and the number of days when the temperature was below 15°C. The average temperature for the 365 days is also output. Give the statements that need to be inserted at A, B, C and D.

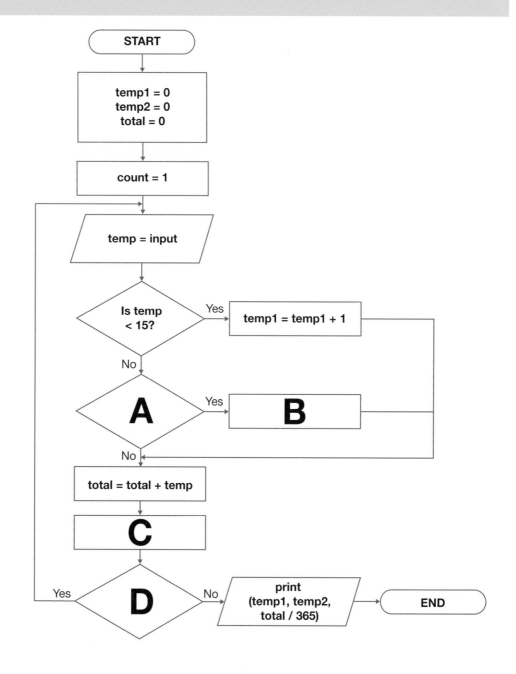

Draw a flow diagram which inputs the top speed of a number of cars (-1 is used to stop the input). The average top speed of all the cars is finally output.

Q19 Draw a flow diagram which outputs the maximum of 10 numbers input by the user.

5.5 – Developing algorithms using pseudocode

Pseudocode is used to write an algorithm in programming-style constructs but it is not in an actual programming language. You do not need to worry about the detailed syntax or be precise about how the code will do something; you just describe the steps you will need in your algorithm.

Basic programming constructs

There are three constructs used to write algorithms in pseudocode (and in actual code):

- sequence
- selection
- iteration

Sequence

Sequence is just a matter of writing the steps down in the order they need to happen. For example:

```
Input the product price
Input the quantity
total = quantity x price
Output "Total price is " + total
```

The statements above are perfectly acceptable pseudocode – it is quite clear what the steps are, and you can write your algorithms using similar statements. However, in an exam you will see more standardised pseudocode statements used, and the four statements above would be written as:

```
productPrice = input ("Please enter product price")
quantity = input ("Please enter quantity")
total = quantity * price
print ("Total price is ", total)
```

The statement `productPrice = input("Please enter product price")` looks rather odd at first – it means 'Display a prompt on the screen, `"Please input product price"` and when the user enters it, assign it in the variable `productPrice`.'

The pseudocode statement in this case is exactly how Python code would be written.

Examples of pseudocode assignments

```
costPrice = 10.0
total = costPrice * 2
gender = "M"
name = "Mike Smith"
option = True
```

Selection

Using an if…then…else statement

The `if…then…else` construct allows you to choose between two options.

```
if x <= 10 then
   z = z + 10
else
   z = z - 10
   y = y + 1
endif
```

Using an if…then statement

You can write an `if…then` statement without an `else`.

```
if gameWon == True then
      (instructions here)
endif
```

Using an if…else if statement

```
if menuChoice == 1 then
   display rules
else if menuChoice == 2 then
   play game
else if menuChoice == 3 then
   exit
endif
```

Nested selection statements

You can also write one or more `if` statements nested inside another selection statement. The following example uses a nested `if` statement.

Example 1

Write an algorithm to input a user name and check if it is equal to MANH123. If it is, input a user password, and check if the password is equal to XYZ123a, otherwise output a message "Invalid user name". If the password is correct, output "Access granted", otherwise, output a message "Invalid password".

```
username = input ("Enter user name")
if username == "MANH123" then
   password = input ("Enter password")
   if password == "XYZ123a" then
     print ("Access granted")
   else
      print ("Invalid password")
   endif
else
   print ("Invalid username")
endif
(continue)
```

Switch/case statement

The **switch/case** statement is designed for coding multiple choices in a program, such as a menu of several options where the user will enter one choice.

```
switch menuChoice of
    case 1: display rules
    case 2: play game
    case 3: exit
else
    print ("Select 1-3: ")
endswitch
```

Iteration

There are three basic iteration (loop) constructs that you will learn when you program.

The **for** loop allows you to execute a group of steps 1 or more times, for a specific number of times.

```
for count = 1 to 10
    print (count * 3)
next count
```

> Not all programming languages use **next n** but we normally use it in algorithms just to be really clear that **count** is incremented each time around the loop.

A **repeat** or **do** loop is controlled by a condition **at the end** of the loop. It will, therefore, always execute the following steps **at least once**. Here is an example of an algorithm that uses a **repeat** loop:

```
count = 1
repeat
    print (count * 3)
    count = count + 1
until count == 10
```

A **while** loop is controlled by a condition **at the start** of the loop. It will, therefore, execute the following steps **zero or more** times. This is important when you read from a file, for example, when you need to make sure the file is not empty **before** you try to read from it. Here is an example of an algorithm that uses a WHILE loop:

```
while not customerfile.endOfFile()
    write count * 3
    count = count + 1
endwhile
```

> **customerfile.endOfFile()** is used to determine the end of the file called **customerFile.**
>
> Not all programming languages use **endwhile** but we normally use it in algorithms to be clear where the loop ends.

Example 7

A computerised form prompts a user to enter their email address.

The validation rules check if the address has an @ symbol in it. If it doesn't, an error message is displayed, the text box is cleared and the system asks the user to enter the email address again. This continues until an appropriate address is entered.

The system then checks that the email address has been typed in lowercase and if not, it converts it to lowercase.

Once the email address is ok it is stored in the customer file.

The flow diagram for this could be as follows:

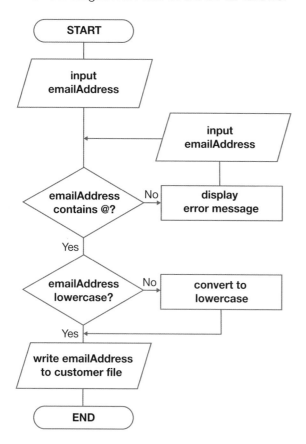

```
emailAddress = input

while not hasAtSign
    print error message
    emailAddress = input
endwhile

if emailAddress is not
lowercase then
    Convert to lowercase
endif

Write emailAddress to
customer file
```

Q20 The **if** statement to check whether the address is lowercase is not needed. Modify the algorithm so that it performs the same task without the **if** statement.

Q21 Write a pseudocode algorithm which inputs 10 numbers. Each time a number less than zero is input, the program displays which number it is, and its value. When all numbers have been input, display the average of all the negative numbers. Your algorithm should allow for the fact that there may be no negative numbers.

Sample output could be, for example:

```
Number 3   -8
Number 7   -20
Average of negative numbers = -14
```

Q22 Write a routine that inputs a series of numbers. Output how many numbers are greater than 60. A dummy value of -1 ends the input.

Q23 Write a routine that inputs a value x and then inputs x numbers. Output how many numbers were negative and how many were positive.

5.6 – Interpret, correct or complete algorithms

Several of the earlier examples of algorithms included a description of what function they are carrying out. One of the best ways of finding out what an algorithm is doing is to produce a trace table. This shows how the value of a variable changes as the algorithm is "run". It can also be used in the **correction** of errors found in the algorithm.

Example 8

Produce a trace table for the following pseudocode algorithm. By inspecting the way in which variable values change, it should be possible to interpret what the algorithm is doing.

```
total = 0
conversion = 128
for count = 1 to 8
    digit = input ("Please enter a digit")
    value = digit * conversion
    total = total + value
    conversion = conversion / 2
next count
print (total)
```

The following digits are input: 1, 1, 0, 1, 1, 0, 1, 0

Count	Digit	Value	Total	Conversion
			0	128
1	1	128	128	64
2	1	64	192	32
3	0	0	192	16
4	1	16	208	8
5	1	8	216	4
6	0	0	216	2
7	1	2	218	1
8	0	0	218	
		OUTPUT:	218	

We can see from this trace table that the algorithm is converting an 8-bit binary number into a base 10 (denary) number.

Notice here the use of **meaningful variable names** which are a key part of understanding or interpreting the function of an algorithm.

Example 9

Look at the following flow diagram and follow through the variable values in the trace table:

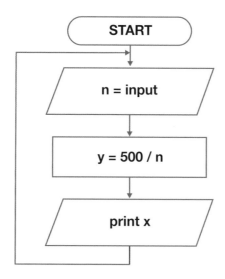

n	y
10	50
1000	0.5
-2	-250
0	ERROR

The trace table for the input values of **10, 1000, -2, 0** indicates that an error will occur when n = 0 is input. The program would "crash" if this input value was encountered.

Dry running an algorithm is a very good way of checking an algorithm before writing the program code. Once the code is written, it can be checked using test data with known outcomes.

Here is a flow diagram for the modified algorithm:

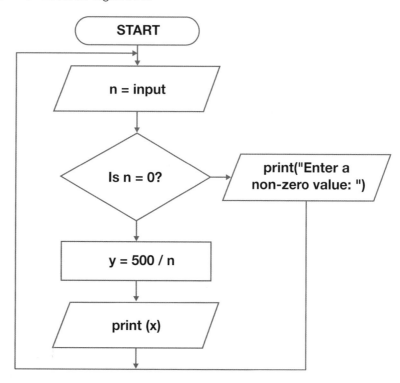

Completion of algorithms

Suppose we want an algorithm to do the following tasks:

- Loop round 100 times to input 100 temperatures
- Output the number of temperatures >= 0 and the number of temperatures < 0
- Output the mean temperature of the 100 input

This is a first attempt at a pseudocode algorithm. (Line numbers are used here to help in the discussion.)

```
10    for count = 1 to 100
20        temperature = input ("Enter temperature")
30        if temperature >= 0 then
40            t1ZeroOrMore = t1ZeroOrMore + 1
50        else
60            t2LessThanZero = t2LessThanZero + 1
70        endif
80    next count
90    print (t1ZeroOrMore, t2LessThanZero)
```

Inspection of this algorithm shows that the following parts are missing:

- Setting all the totals to 0 initially
- Summation of all 100 temperatures to allow the mean value to be determined
- Outputting the mean temperature

Here is the modified algorithm with the extra lines inserted:

```
5     t1ZeroOrMore = 0
6     t2LessThanZero = 0
7     totalTemp = 0
10    for count = 1 to 100
20        input temperature
30        if temperature >= 0 then
40            t1ZeroOrMore = t1ZeroOrMore + 1
50        else
60            t2LessThanZero = t2LessThanZero + 1
70        endif
75        totalTemp = totalTemp + temperature
80    next count
90    print (t1ZeroOrMore, t2LessThanZero)
95    meanTemperature = totalTemp/100
96    print meanTemperature
```

You may be asked to complete an algorithm based on the original task description and an inspection of the algorithm to see if it fulfils its tasks.

In a real situation, completion of an algorithm could be carried out by a different analyst or it could even be done several months later in the process, so using meaningful variable names and indentation is important.

Q24 Complete the trace table for the following algorithm and state its function.

```
total = 0
for count = 1 to 4
    base = input ("Enter base: ")
    height = input ("Enter height: ")
    value = (base * height) * 0.5
    total = total + value
next count
print (total / 4)
```

Use the following input values: 10, 20, 8, 6, 16, 12, 15, 40

Total	Count	Base	Height	value
0	1	10	20	100

Q25 What does the following algorithm do?

```
item = [34, 26, 37, 12, 73, 11, 47, 29]
n = number of items in list
for i = 0 to n - 2
    for j = 0 to n - i - 2
        if item[j] > item[j + 1] then
            swap the items
        endif
    next j
next i
```

Complete the pseudocode for "swap the items".

Exercises

1. **Abstraction** and **decomposition** are two aspects of computational thinking.

   (a) Sienna is designing a program to control a cat-flap which will open only when a cat approaches.

   Describe two ways in which she may use abstraction in reaching a solution to this problem. [2]

   (b) A program is required to enter a set of students' examination marks, count the number of students who obtained each mark and output the counts for each mark. Examination marks entered must be in the range 0 to 500.

   Explain how **decomposition** might be used in designing a solution to this problem. [3]

2. (a) A **binary search** is used to search for integers in the following list:

    3, 6, 7, 10, 14, 16, 19, 22, 24, 27, 29, 36, 45, 47, 50, 51, 53

    Which items will be examined when searching for:

    (i)   6   [2]

    (ii) 53   [2]

    (b) (i)   A bubble sort is used to sort the following numbers:

        34, 56, 89, 23, 12, 77, 49, 44

        What order will the numbers be in after the first pass?   [2]

    (ii) How many passes will be required to sort the items?   [1]

    (c) A **merge sort** is to be used to sort the same numbers. During the merge phase, the
    following 4 pairs of numbers need to be merged back into two groups of four.

    (34, 56), (23, 89), (12, 77), (44,49)

    What will be the contents of each group of four numbers after the next phase of the
    merge?   [2]

3. A school uses a computer program to give every new pupil a username for logging onto
    computers. The algorithm used to choose the username is shown below.

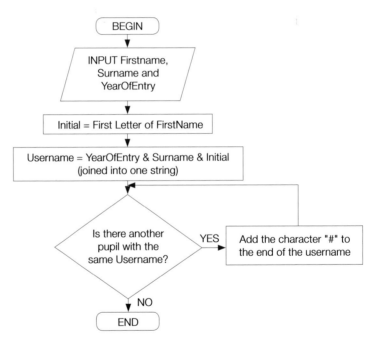

    (a) Mark Johnson joins the school in 2012. No other pupil called Johnson joins the school in
    the same year.

    State the username which Mark will be given and explain how you obtained your answer
    from the flow diagram.   [3]

    (b) A pupil has the username 2010alim###.

    State **four** facts that we can work out from this username.   [4]

OCR A451 June 2012 Qu 8

4. An isosceles triangle is a triangle that has at least two equal length sides. The diagram below shows examples of isosceles triangles. In each diagram the marked sides are equal.

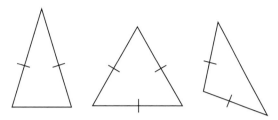

Write an algorithm for a computer program that determines whether a triangle is an isosceles triangle.

- The user inputs the lengths of the three sides as Length1, Length2 and Length3
- If any two sides have the same length the program outputs "Isosceles"
- Otherwise the program outputs "Not Isosceles"   [5]

OCR A451 June 2013 Qu 10

5. The following algorithm (written in pseudocode) is intended to input ten numbers and output the largest number input and the average value of the ten numbers.

```
10    largest = 0
20    sum = 0
30    for x = 1 to 40
40       x = input("Input x: ")
50            if x > largest then x = largest
60       print (largest)
70       sum = sum + x
80    endif
90    next x
100   average = sum * 10

110   print (average)
```

There are at least **four** errors in this algorithm.

(a) Locate the errors in the algorithm.   [4]

(b) Rewrite the algorithm so that it works as intended.   [6]

6. Look at this flow diagram and then draw and complete a trace table using the input data supplied and the headings given below for the trace table. [6]

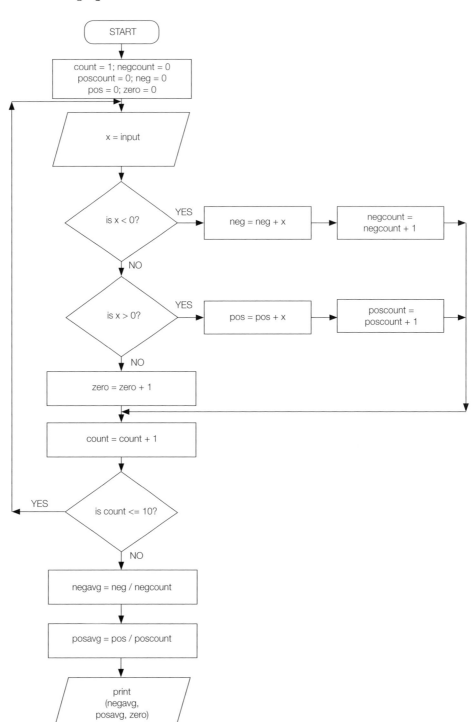

0, 8, 7, 10, -8, -7, 0, 0, -3, 11

x	neg	negcount	pos	poscount	zero	count	count<=10	negavg	posavg	Output

Section 6

Programming

Objectives

- Use data types: integer, real, Boolean, character and string

- Use casting to change a variable type

- Use constants and variables

- Use input, output and assignment statements

- Use the common arithmetic operators including mod and div

- Use string manipulation functions

- Use programming constructs sequence, selection and iteration

- Combine common Boolean operators using AND, OR, NOT to two levels

- Use one- and two-dimensional arrays

- Use records to store data

- Use SQL to search for data

- Use sub-programs (functions and procedures) to produce structured code

- Use basic file-handling operations: open, read, write, close

6

6.1 – Programming concepts

Variables and data types

Any data that a program uses must be stored in main memory locations, each given its own identifier while the program is running. As the program runs, the values in these locations might change, which is why they are called **variables**. For example: a variable called `total` might change several times as many numbers are added to it. A variable called `surname` may change as the program processes a list of customer orders.

Each variable has an **identifier** (a unique name) that refers to a location in memory where the data item will be stored. Each variable also has a **data type** that defines the type of data that will be stored at the memory location and therefore the operations that can be performed on it (for example, you can multiply two numbers but you can't multiply two words).

Declaring variables

In some programming languages variables are declared at the start of a program so that when the program runs, the appropriate amount of memory can be reserved to store the data. The following are examples from a Visual Basic program:

```
dim num1 as integer
dim total as single
dim choice as char
dim username as string
dim found as Boolean
```

In any high-level language where you declare variables, the statement will include an **identifier** and a **data type**.

In some languages, for example Python, you do not declare variables at all. The program will assume the data type of a variable based on what is put in it. So if you write `a = 23`, `b = "Fred"`, a will be stored as an integer (whole number) and b will be stored as a string (text).

Even if you do not have to declare variables in your particular programming language, you need to understand the different data types and how to work with them in the programs you write.

The table below shows a list of some data types and the typical amount of memory that each needs.

Data Type	Type of Data	Typical Amount of Memory
integer	A whole number, such as 3, 45, -453	2 or 4 bytes
real/float	A number with a fractional part such as 34.456, -9.234, or 4.0	4 or 8 bytes
char/character	A single character, where a character can be any letter, digit, punctuation mark or symbol that can be typed	1 byte
string	Zero or more characters. A string can be null (empty), just one character or several characters	1 byte per character in the string
Boolean	A Boolean variable has the value True or False	1 byte

The programming language that you are using may have different names for some of these, for example, "real" is called "float" in some languages. Your language will also have some additional data types not listed. The amount of memory used for each data type also varies for different programming languages; for example, an integer may need 2 bytes in one language but 4 bytes in another.

Assignment statements

Values are assigned to variables using an = sign. For example:

```
x = 1
pi = 3.242
alpha = "a"
street = "Elm Street"
over18 = True
```

Constants

In some programs, there are certain values that remain the same (constant) while the program runs. The programmer could use the actual value in the code each time, but it is good practice to give the value a unique name (an **identifier**) and then use that name throughout the program. **Constants** are declared at the start of a program and can then be referred to as needed in the code. For example:

Please note, though, this does not mean that the constant's value will never change during the

At the start of the program: CONST **VATRate** = 0.2;

Later in the program code: sellPrice = netPrice * **VATRate** + netPrice;

lifetime of the system! For example, the VAT rate will stay the same (constant) while the program runs in the shop each day but, after the next budget, it may change. The value allocated to that constant will then need to be edited in the program.

The two main benefits of declaring a constant are:

- When its value changes, you only have to edit it in one place rather than looking for every place in the program where you used that value
- The code will be easier to read and understand because the constant's identifier will be used instead of a number. This makes your code easier to debug and, later on, maintain.

In some languages such as Python, there is no special way to declare constants at the start of the program. You just write an assignment statement such as

VATRATE = 0.2

By convention, in Python the identifier of a constant is written in uppercase, which makes it clear that this is a value which should not be changed within the code.

Input and output statements

Example 1

Write pseudocode for a program that asks the user to input their name. It accepts a name, for example John and then displays Hello John on the screen.

```
myName = input("Please enter your name: ")
print("Hello " myName)
```

The first statement displays on the screen

```
Please enter your name:
```

and waits for the user to enter something. If the user types `John`, the print statement then displays on the screen

```
Hello John
```

The first statement could be written as two separate statements:

```
print("Please enter your name: ")
myName = input()
```

However, we will generally use one statement to display a prompt and accept user input.

Operations on data

Operations are things you can do to specific types of data. For example, you can perform arithmetic operations on numbers and you can perform string-handling operations on text.

Numerical data types

Operations that can be performed on numerical data types are as follows:

Arithmetic operations *(give a numerical result)*		**Comparison operations** *(give a boolean result: true or false)*	
eg: 25 + 3 = 28		eg: 456 > 34 is true	
+	(addition)	<	(less than)
-	(subtraction)	>	(greater than)
*	(multiplication)	<=	(less than or equal to)
/	(division)	>=	(greater than or equal to)
^	(exponentiation)	!= or <>	(not equal to)
DIV or //	(integer division)	== or =	(equal to)
MOD or %	(modulus)		

The arithmetic operators and the Boolean operators vary slightly between different programming languages. In OCR pseudocode, where there are differences, the first option will be used in exam questions.

When performing operations on data items you need to consider the data types used. For example, in a simple calculation where two whole numbers are added together, variables in Pascal could be defined as follows:

```
Var
    num1, num2, total : integer;
```

But if the calculation involves division, then the answer variable should be declared as a real number:

```
Var
    num1, num2 : integer;
    answer     : real;
```

The arithmetic operators DIV and MOD can only be performed on whole numbers (integers).

DIV is integer division. It works like normal division but returns the whole number of times one number goes into the other. Here are some examples:

```
13 DIV 3 = 4
30 DIV 3 = 10
32 DIV 3 = 10
```

MOD gives the remainder of integer division as follows:

```
13 MOD 3 = 1
30 MOD 3 = 0
32 MOD 3 = 2
```

The exponentiation operator calculates the power of a number, so for example $7^2 = 49$

> **Q1** State the values of w, x, y and z that will be output when these statements are executed:
>
> ```
> w = 54
> x = w mod 7
> y = x div 2
> z = y^3
> print(w, x, y, z)
> ```

Casting

Casting means changing the type of a variable value from one type to another. This is done with functions such as `int()`, `float()` or `str()`.

Changing a string to an integer

You may need to convert a string to a number so that you can use it in a calculation. Python, for example, accepts all user input as strings, not numbers.

Consider the following program in Python:

```
num1 = input ("Please enter first number")
num2 = input ("Please enter second number")
num3 = num1 + num2
print("The sum is ", num3)
```

If the user enters 3 and 5, you would expect `num3` to be 8. However, the program outputs

```
The sum is 35
```

What has happened? The numbers are input as strings, and the + symbol when used with strings means **concatenation**, or joining the two strings together.

You need to convert each of the strings to integers or floating point numbers. A corrected program would look like this:

```
num1 = int(input("Please enter first number"))
num2 = int(input("Please enter second number"))
num3 = num1 + num2
print("The sum is ", num3)
```

The `int` function changes the variable type to an integer.

The `float` function changes a string variable to a floating point number:

```
price = float(input("Please enter price: "))
```

> **Q2** Write pseudocode for a program which asks the user to enter a first name and surname, and prints out the whole name.

Changing an integer to a floating point number

If you divide an integer by another integer, and end up with a floating point number, Python will automatically convert the result to a floating point number for you. However, in a programming language which requires you to declare variables and their types before using them, you should declare the result of a division as a floating point (real) number.

```
num1 = 10
num2 = 3
num3 = num1/num2
print(num3)
```

will print 3.33333333333333 or something similar.

In summary: (Note the use of quote marks to define strings.)

```
str(27)         returns    "27"
str(4.7)        returns    "4.7"
int("27")       returns    27
float("5.67")   returns    5.67
```

> **Q3** Write pseudocode for a program that asks the user to enter the total amount of a restaurant bill, divides it by 5 and prints out what each person owes.

6 String manipulation

A string is anything enclosed in quote marks. Programming languages have built-in **functions** to manipulate strings.

The functions given below are given in a generalised format which you may see in pseudocode. Each programming language will have its own particular functions and syntax.

To get the length of a string:

```
stringname.length
```

To get a substring:

```
stringname.substring(startingPosition, numberOfCharacters)
```

(It is assumed on this course that a string starts at position 0, not 1, so `stringname[0]` contains the first character of a string called `stringname`.)

To convert cases:

```
stringname.upper
stringname.lower
```

To find the position of a character or the start of a string:

```
stringname.index("son")
```

Example 2

In the statements below, the result of each operation is shown in a comment on the right. In the pseudocode that we will be using, all comments will start with the characters //.

```
myName = "John Robinson"
firstname = myName.substring(0, 3)              // "John"
surname = myName.substring(5, 7)                // "Rob"
numChars = myName.length                        // 13
lastTwoChars = myName.substring(numChars - 2, 2) // "on"
positionOfRob = myName.index ("Rob")            // 5
```

Q4 Write pseudocode to assign the number 5387026 to an integer variable. Convert this to a string, and print out the number of digits in the integer and the middle three digits.

Q5 Write pseudocode to accept a first name and surname from the user, which may be entered in lowercase or uppercase. Print the initials in uppercase, separated by a space.

Converting characters to and from ASCII

Every character is represented in binary, for example using the ASCII representation. ASCII, "A" is represented by the same binary code as the decimal number 65, "B" is 66, "C" is 67,... "Z" is 90.

The functions **ord** (or **asc**) and **chr** convert characters between ASCII and decimal.

```
num = ord("A")    // puts num = 65
letter = chr(66)  // puts letter = "B"
```

Q6 Write pseudocode statements to accept a character from the user, convert it to uppercase, and output the next character in the alphabet. If the user inputs z, "A" should be output.

6.2 – Sequence and selection

In Section 5 the basic program structures of sequence, selection and iteration were briefly covered. In this section the use of these structures will be looked at in more detail, with examples of more complex algorithms.

Sequence

All programs have a series of steps to be followed in sequence. Here is an example in which the steps are simple assignment statements:

Example 3

```
score1 = int(input("Enter score for Round 1: ")
score2 = int(input("Enter score for Round 2: ")
print("The average score is ", (score1 + score2)/2)
```

Or, the sequence may be a series of calls to different subroutines which perform different tasks. Subroutines (functions and procedures) will be covered in Section 6.5.

Selection

Before looking at algorithms using the different selection statements available in a programming language, we need to take a closer look at Boolean data types and expressions, since these are used to determine which path through the program will be taken.

Boolean data type

Boolean variables are either True or False. It makes no sense to perform mathematical operations on them or to compare them to see which is greater. With Boolean variables we use **logical operators** to create **Boolean expressions**. Logical operations you should know are:

NOT   AND   OR

Boolean expressions

Boolean expressions are used to control selection statements. For example:

```
if score > 30 then
    print("Well done")
```

A complex Boolean expression contains one or more of the operators **AND**, **OR** or **NOT**.
For example:

```
if (X ≤ 10) OR (CurrentCharNum > LengthOfString) then …
```

Consider an estate agent's program that searches through a file of house details to find ones that match a customer's requirements. In this case the customer wants a house or flat, but it must have more than three bedrooms:

```
if (Rooms > 3) AND ((type == "House") OR (type == "Flat")) then
    Output details
endif
```

Notice the extra set of brackets around the second half of the expression. AND takes precedence over OR so without the extra brackets the program would return all the houses with more than three bedrooms as well as any flats, whether they have more than three bedrooms or not.

> **Q7**   Write pseudocode statements to check whether a username entered by the user is equal to either "User1" or "User2". If so, print "Access granted", otherwise print "Access denied".

Writing robust code

Robust code is code which will not result in the program crashing due to an unexpected user input. The pseudocode given above in Example 3 for calculating an average of two scores would crash for some inputs. Why? The algorithm needs to be amended so that it will not crash whatever the user enters.

```
score1 = int(input("Enter score for Round 1: ")
score2 = int(input("Enter score for Round 2: ")
if (score1 == 0) AND (score2 == 0) then
    print("The average score is 0")
else
    print("The average score is ", (x + y)/2)
endif
```

Example 4

A room is to be carpeted using carpet that is 4m wide. The program asks the user to enter the room dimensions, and if both width and length are greater than 3.9m, prints out "wider carpet required". Otherwise, it calculates the length of carpet required by adding 2% to the length of the room.

The following algorithm has been written:

```
roomLength = input("Enter room length: ")
roomWidth = input("Enter room width: ")
if roomLength > 3.9 then
    print ("Carpet not wide enough")
else
    carpetLength = roomLength * 1.02
    print("Length of carpet required = ", carpetLength)
endif
```

The algorithm contains an error. Can you find it?

Even if the program did not contain an error, it could still give the wrong answer if the user did not enter the longest dimension as the length. The program needs to check for this. Here is the rewritten algorithm:

```
roomLength = input("Enter room length: ")
roomWidth = input("Enter room width: ")
if (roomLength < roomWidth) AND (roomWidth > 3.9) then
    temp = roomLength
    roomLength = roomWidth
    roomWidth = temp
endif
if roomWidth > 3.9 then
    print("Carpet not wide enough")
else
    carpetLength = roomLength * 1.02
    print("Length of carpet required = ", carpetLength)
endif
```

 Q8 In Section 5, you learned how to write complex selection statements using either a `case` statement or a nested `if` statement

Write an algorithm to solve the following problem:

- If a student gets A* in GCSE Maths, he or she will be advised to consider taking Further Maths at A Level
- If a student gets A in GCSE Maths, he or she will be advised to consider taking Maths at A Level
- If a student gets B in GCSE Maths, he or she will be advised to consider taking Maths at AS Level
- Otherwise, they will be advised not to continue with Maths.

6

Q9 Julie has written an algorithm in the form of a flow diagram for a dice game played with three dice. When the player rolls the dice, they are given points according to the rules shown in the flow diagram.

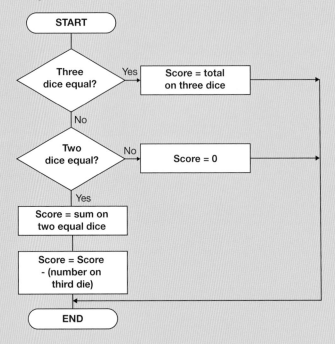

(a) Show the value of the score if the dice rolled are: (i) 2 4 6   (ii) 5 5 5   (iii) 2 2 3

(b) State a set of numbers which will result in a negative score.

(c) Write a selection statement which will test if all three dice are equal.

6.3 – Iteration

Frequently, sections of code need to be repeated a certain number of times, or until a certain condition is true or false.

For...**next**, **while**...**endwhile** and **repeat**...**until** are three different types of iterative statement. Note that they are not always all available in a given programming language.

The for... next loop

This type of loop is useful when you know how many times the loop is to be repeated. For example, if you are drawing a square on a screen using a turtle, you could use the following algorithm:

```
for n == 1 to 4
    draw line
    turn 90 degrees
next n
```

Suppose you need to write an algorithm which gives a user exactly three attempts to enter their username correctly. You can assume the computer has the correct user name in a variable called correctName.

A first go at writing the algorithm might be:

```
accessGranted = False
for attempt == 1 to 3
   username = input("Please enter username: ")
   if (username != correctName) then
      username = input ("Incorrect username - please re-enter: ")
   else
      accessGranted = True
   endif
next attempt
```

One problem with this algorithm, as you probably spotted, is that even if the user enters the correct username on the first attempt, they are still asked to enter it again a second and third time.

Q10   Can you find and correct the second error in the algorithm?

The while…endwhile loop

The expression in the while statement controlling the repetition must be a Boolean condition which evaluates to True or False.

The expression is tested at the **start** of the loop.

This means that sometimes the statements inside the loop are not executed at all.

Boolean expressions are used to control this type of loop. For example:

```
while reply != "compScience"
   reply = input("Please re-enter password")
endwhile
```

You may sometimes need complex Boolean expressions, for example:

```
while (NOT A > B) AND (NOT ItemFound) …
```

6

Q11   Write pseudocode statements to allow a user three attempts to enter the correct password, "compScience".

Example 5

We can rewrite the algorithm given above using a while…endwhile loop.

```
accessGranted = False
attempt = 1
userName = input("Please enter username: ")
while (attempt <= 3) AND (accessGranted == False)
   if (userName != correctName) then
      if (attempt < 3) then
         userName = input("Incorrect username - please re-enter: ")
      endif
      attempt = attempt + 1
   else
      accessGranted = True
   endif
endwhile
```

A `while...endwhile` loop is also useful when allowing a user to continue entering data until they indicate there is no more data to enter by inputting a "dummy" value. Here is an algorithm which allows a user to continue entering values until a dummy value of xxx is entered.

```
total = 0
markstring = input("Please enter next mark, xxx to end: ")
while markstring != "xxx"
    mark = int(markstring)
    total = total + mark
    markstring = input("Please enter next mark, xxx to end: ")
endwhile
print("Total of all marks: ", total)
```

Q12 Write an algorithm which allows a user to enter daily temperatures and when the user enters xxx, outputs the maximum and average temperature.

Repeat...until loop

This loop differs from the `while...endwhile` loop in that it tests the loop condition at the **end** of the loop rather than at the beginning. It is therefore always performed at least once.

You may have seen pseudocode using a `repeat` loop to carry on until the user typed N or n. The loop would look something like this with the condition at the end:

```
repeat
...
until (continue == "N") OR (continue == 'n')
```

Example 6

Write a program which tests someone on powers of 2 up to 2^{12}.

```
//random(a,b) generates a random integer between a and b
repeat
    power = random(2,12)
    powerOf2 = 2^power
    answer = input("What is 2 to the power of " power)
    if answer = powerOf2 then
        print("Correct, well done")
    else
        print("No, it is ",powerOf2)
    endif
    anotherGo = input("Another go? Answer Y or N: ")
    anotherGo = anotherGo.upper() //converts anotherGo to uppercase
until anotherGo == "N"
```

Q13 Rewrite this algorithm using a `while...endwhile` loop.

Nested loops

You can have one loop nested inside another.

Example 7

This algorithm displays all the multiplication tables between 2 and 12.

```
for table = 2 to 12
  for count = 1 to 12
    product = table * count
    print(table, " x ", count, " = ", product)
  next count
next table
```

Q14   What will be the third line output by this algorithm?

6.4 – Arrays

We have said that all the variables needed in a program are held in main memory. If we were processing one or two specific data items, then we would have a different identifier for each of these. For example, a program that adds two numbers together might use variables called num1, num2 and total, all of type integer.

Often a program will process a number of data items of the same type, for example if it is sorting a list of 1000 student names.

We could use variables called student1, student2, student3, ... student1000 to store the names but programming languages allow you to use an **array** (or list) to make processing groups of data easier to code. An array is a group of data items of the same data type, which is stored under one identifier (name) in contiguous (one after another) memory locations.

1-dimensional arrays

This program processes 12 numbers using a simple array of integers called score. Imagine a table with one row of 12 boxes:

```
           0   1   2   3   4   5   6   7   8   9   10  11
          ┌───┬───┬───┬───┬───┬───┬───┬───┬───┬───┬───┬───┐
 score:   │   │   │   │   │   │   │   │   │   │   │   │   │
          └───┴───┴───┴───┴───┴───┴───┴───┴───┴───┴───┴───┘
```

Each box in the table can contain an integer. Each box has a numerical reference called a **subscript** or **index** that is used to refer to that individual data item. Note that the first element of the array shown here has a subscript of zero. For example, the third box in this array is referred to as score[2].

In some languages the subscript starts at 1, and at the start of a program the array is defined, just as a variable would be. For example, in Delphi the index can start at 0 or 1, so the array could be declared as:

```
score: array [1..12] of integer;
```

However, in the pseudocode used in this book, all arrays will have subscripts starting at 0.

The individual boxes in the array can be used just like variables:

- **Assign** values to them: `score[4] = 27`

- **Input** values into them from the keyboard or a file:

  ```
  score[4] = input("Enter score: ")
  ```

- **Output** the value stored in a box to the screen or a file:

  ```
  print("The fourth value is ", score[3])
  ```

The benefits of using arrays are:

- Code is easier to follow and therefore easier to debug and maintain

- A group of data items can be easily processed using a `for` loop

When you process data held in an array, you typically do the same thing to each data item, so having them stored in numbered locations makes this much easier and quicker to code.

Example 8

The following algorithm initialises each element of an array to zero, then gets 12 numbers from the user, adds them up and outputs the total:

```
total = 0
for game = 0 to 11
    score[game] = input("Enter number: ")
    total = total + score[game]
next game
print("Total is ", total)
```

Q15 Write an algorithm which inputs ten names into an array, converts each name to uppercase, sorts them into alphabetical order and prints them out. You may assume that a method `sort` exists which will sort an array into ascending order. The statements

```
oldList = [6, 4, 9, 24, 36, 1, 4]
newList = oldList.sort()
```

will make `newlist` equal to `[1, 4, 4, 6, 9, 24, 36]`

2-dimensional arrays

Suppose you need to store 10 test scores for each of a class of 30 students. You could use a 2-dimensional array called `classScores`, which would, for example, hold the 5th test score for the 2nd student in `classScores[1][4]`. (Remember the array indices start at 0.)

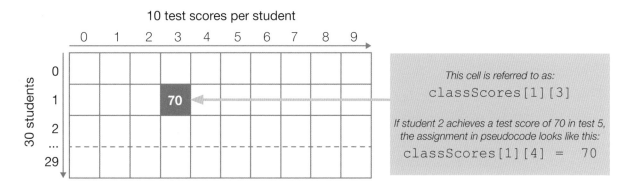

10 test scores per student

This cell is referred to as:
`classScores[1][3]`

If student 2 achieves a test score of 70 in test 5, the assignment in pseudocode looks like this:
`classScores[1][4] = 70`

Example 9

Write an algorithm to allow the user to enter the 10 test scores for each student, and calculate and output the average mark obtained by each student.

The student names are held in an array `studentName[29]` so that for example `student[0]` contains the name `Adams J.`

An array `total[29]` will hold the total marks for each student.

An array `average[29]` will hold the average mark for each student.

The program prompts the user: `"Enter 10 marks for Adams J"` and then stores the mark input by the user.

```
# initialize array to hold total marks
for n = 0 to 29
   total[n] = 0
endfor
#input names and marks
for name = 0 to 29
   print("Enter marks for ", studentName[n])
   for mark = 0 to 9
      classScores[name][mark] = input
      total[name] = total[name] + classScores[name][mark]
   endfor
endfor
for n = 0 to 29
   average[n] = total[n] / 10
   print(studentName[n], average[n])
endfor
```

6

> **Q16** Write an algorithm which allows a user to enter a student number, and which then outputs their name, each of their 10 scores and their average score. You may assume the data for each student has been entered into the arrays using the algorithm given above.
>
> Remember that the array indices start at 0, but the students will be numbered 1 to 30 in the teacher's record book. So if the teacher enters 3 for the student number, that student's name will be found in `studentName[2]` in the program.

> **Q17** Quarterly sales (in £000s) for each of six supermarkets are held in a two-dimensional array `sales` which has 6 rows and 4 columns. Write an assignment statement to assign the value 150 to Store 5 for the third quarter sales.

6.5 – Procedures and functions

A **subroutine** or **sub-program** is a named self-contained section of code that performs a specific task.

Imagine a recipe for a lemon meringue pie. You could have the recipe written out in one long list of instructions but it might be easier to separate out instructions for making pastry and making meringue, especially as these same instructions will be used in several other recipes as well.

The recipe for Lemon Meringue Pie might say:

1. Make short-crust pastry (see Recipe 5)
2. Make the meringue (see Recipe 12)
3. Mix the lemon rind, sugar etc.

Programs are similar. If you have some code that does a specific task, it can be written as a self-contained subroutine. It can then be used from anywhere in the program as needed, without writing all the instructions out again and again.

In a system that has several parts to it, perhaps selected from a menu, it is much easier to write and debug your code if it is written in subroutines. The main program might be a `switch` statement that calls the subroutines to process each menu choice. This is pseudocode but will look similar in your language:

```
switch choice:
    case 1: AddNewCar
    case 2: FindCarDetails
    case 3: ListCarsByMake
endswitch
```

You can see from this example that using subroutines makes the program structure really clear. Another benefit is that each subroutine can be written and tested in isolation from the other modules. This makes debugging much easier and, in the future, the program will be easier to maintain.

Procedures

There are two different types of subroutine, called **procedures** and **functions**. We will look first at procedures.

Defining a procedure

This procedure prints a greeting.

```
procedure greeting
    print("Hello")
    print("You're looking well")
endprocedure
```

To call this procedure, you write the name of the procedure wherever you want to call it.

```
greeting
```

Receiving information through parameters

To make the procedure more useful, you can pass it one or more **parameters**. The parameter is a variable named in the procedure heading that will receive and use whatever value you pass it.

```
procedure greeting(name)
   print("Hello", name)
   print("You're looking well")
endprocedure
```

To call this procedure, you write the name of the procedure wherever you want to call it, and specify what parameter is to be used.

```
greeting("James")
greeting("Helen")
firstname = input("What is your name? ")
greeting(firstname)
```

When this program is run, it will print

```
Hello James
You're looking well
Hello Helen
You're looking well
What is your name?
(user enters a name, e.g. Kerry)
Hello Kerry
You're looking well
```

You can pass as many parameters as you like, separated by commas.

> Write a procedure that accepts two parameters for oven temperature and number of eggs and prints out, for example, "Set the oven to 180 degrees. You will need 3 eggs."
>
> Write instructions to call the procedure with two different sets of data.

Functions

Functions are similar to procedures; they are self-contained sections of code. The key difference is that they always return a value.

We have already used several built-in functions such as **asc** and **chr:**

```
letter = chr(68)           // assigns "D" to letter
asciiValue = asc("B")      // assigns 66 to asciiValue
```

Example 10

Here is a sample function written in pseudocode to convert centimetres to inches:

```
function cms2inches(metric)
   conversionFactor = 2.54
   inches =  metric / conversionFactor
   return inches
endfunction
```

The subroutine in this case contains a `return` statement, which identifies it as a function rather than a procedure.

It could be used in a line of code like this:

```
HeightMetric = input("Enter your height in centimetres: ")
print("Your height in inches is ", cms2inches(HeightMetric))
```

Write a function to accept two numbers and return the maximum.

Using random number generation functions

A useful function which most programming languages have in their library of functions, is one which will generate a random number within a certain range. Random numbers are frequently used in games programs and in simulations. For example, if you wanted to simulate throwing a die, you could use a function (or strictly speaking, a method) to generate a random number between 1 and 6.

A **method** is called somewhat differently from a **function**, but performs a similar job. When you start doing object-oriented programming (probably not on this course), you will learn more about methods. On this course, you will be told how to write a function or method to perform a particular task so it is not necessary to go into details!

The random number method may be called with a statement such as

```
throw = random.randint(1,6)
```

Example 11

The following algorithm prints a random name from a list of names. The method

```
name = random.choice(names)
```

returns a random element from the list names. You have already come across the method

```
names.index
```

which returns the index position of the start of a string.

```
nameList = ["Anne", "Bob", "Jane", "Vera", "Mabel", "Tony", "Nur"]
totals = [0, 0, 0, 0, 0, 0, 0]
numTimes = int(input("How many names do you want to generate? "))
for i = 1 to numTimes
   index = random.randint(1,7)
   totals[index] = totals[index] + 1
next i
for i = 1 to 7
   print (nameList[i], totals[i])
next i
```

Q20 (a) Approximately how many times would you expect each name to be chosen if the user types 700 for the number of random names to choose?

(b) What is the purpose of the int function in the following line?

```
numTimes = int(input("How many names do you want to
generate? "))
```

(c) Why is it needed in a language such as Python?

Local and global variables

Variables declared or used in the main program are known as **global variables**, and they will be recognised throughout the program and any subroutines that it calls.

Functions and procedures may use their own variables which are not known about or recognised outside the subroutine. In the function in Example 10 which converts centimetres to inches, `conversionFactor` is declared within the subroutine and only exists while the function is being executed. It is not recognised anywhere else in the program.

Here is a function which returns the average of three numbers `n1`, `n2` and `n3`.

```
function average(n1, n2, n3)
   total = n1 + n2 + n3
   avg = total / 3
   return avg
endfunction
```

The function could be called using the statement

```
mean = average(n1, n2, n3)
```

The variable `total` is a local variable inside the function `average`. If you try to print it outside the function, you will get an error message.

> **Q21** Study the algorithm below and answer the questions.
>
> ```
> global pi = 3.142
> function calcArea(radius)
>  area = pi * radius * radius
> endfunction
>
> radius = input("Please enter radius: ")
> calcArea(radius)
> print("Area of the circle is ", area)
> ```
>
> (a) Give an example of a local variable and a global variable in this program.
> (b) What will be the first statement to be executed?
> (c) Explain why last line (the print instruction) will produce an error.
> (d) Correct the algorithm.

Advantages of using subroutines

Using subroutines to perform specific tasks in a program has many advantages.

- Breaking down or **decomposing** a large problem into sub-tasks, and writing each of these as a subroutine, makes the problem easier to solve
- Each subroutine can be **tested** separately
- Subroutines can be used several times within a program
- Subroutines can be stored in a **subroutine library** and used in different programs when needed
- Several programmers can work on a large program at the same time, writing different subroutines, so a large job will get done more quickly
- If the requirements of a problem change, it is much easier just to make a change in a subroutine than to search through a long program to find what lines need changing, so program **maintenance** is easier.

6.6 – Records and files

Earlier in the chapter we looked at arrays. An array is a collection of data items stored under one identifier so that the data items can be processed easily. When we group data items together so they can be treated as a set of data, we refer to this as a **data structure**.

The pseudocode programs we have looked at so far have all used variables which are stored in memory. Often, however, the data needs to be stored in a **file** which can be held permanently on disk, from where it can be read next time it is needed.

Records

Most languages will allow you to define arrays quite easily but sometimes we want to define our own data structures. Imagine a program for a car sales showroom. If your program is going to process details about cars, it will be easier to create a record structure to hold all of the car details rather than storing them as one long string of text or lots of separate variables. We cannot put them in an array because the separate data items we need to store about each car are not all of the same data type.

Here is a text file with some car details in it:

```
RE05 HSD, Ford, 2005, 97500, 650
SW12 SDF, Vauxhall, 2012, 59650, 2500
BN64 WJR, Nissan, 2014, 39900, 18000
```

We could process this file as lines of text but it would be easier it we defined our own data type that gave this line of text some structure. In Delphi a programmer could define this record type as follows:

```
type TCar = record
  registrationNum:     string[8];
  make:                string[15];
  year:                integer;
  mileage:             integer;
  price:               integer;
end;
```

Individual data items within a record are called fields.

In a database, records are shown in a table like the one below:

Table: CarTable

Registration	Make	Year	Mileage	Price
AV60 HES	Peugeot	2010	33156	£5,500
GF56 RTE	Toyota	2006	26875	£8,500
FD02 YOU	Hyundai	2002	85300	£3,499
AD62 HGF	Peugeot	2012	50887	£7,649
AF63 HTE	Peugeot	2013	45860	£6,780
GF64 NGB	Renault	2014	38665	£6,199
GR11 JUL	Renault	2011	90760	£2,999

Using SQL to search for data

Records in this format can be searched using a Structured Query Language (SQL).

The format of an SQL statement is

SELECT... list the field(s) you want displayed here
FROM... list the table or tables the data will come from here
WHERE... list search criteria here

Example 12

Use an SQL statement to find the Year, Mileage and Price of all Peugeot cars

SELECT year, mileage, price
FROM CarTable
WHERE make = "Peugeot"
This will produce the following results:

Year	Mileage	Price
2010	33156	£5,500
2012	50887	£7,649
2013	45860	£6,780

You can use more complex Boolean conditions in the WHERE clause, using AND, and OR.

Example 13

Use an SQL statement to find the Year, Mileage and Price of all Peugeot cars with a net selling price of less than £7,000.

SELECT Year, Mileage, NetSellingPrice
FROM CarTable
WHERE Make = "Peugeot" AND NetSellingPrice < 7000
This will produce the following results:

Year	Mileage	Price
2010	33156	£5,500
2013	45860	£6,780

The Boolean condition LIKE is used with a wildcard character.

The wildcard "%" is a substitute for zero or more characters

The wildcard "*" is a substitute for "all fields"

Example 14

Use an SQL statement to find all fields of all with a registration beginning with the letters "GF"

SELECT *
FROM CarTable
WHERE registration LIKE "GF%"
This will produce the following results:

Registration	Make	Year	Mileage	Price
GF56 RTE	Toyota	2013	26875	£8,500
GF59 NGB	Renault	2014	38665	£6,199

6

Write SQL statements to find:

(i) The make, year and price of all cars with a mileage less than £50,000

(ii) All fields for Renault and Peugeot cars

Handling text files

The pseudocode programs we have looked at so far have all used variables which are stored in memory. Often, however, the data needs to be stored in a **file** which can be held permanently on disk, from where it can be read next time it is needed.

Text files contain text that is in lines. There is no other structure, unlike files of records. When you read from a text file you can only read a whole line at a time. When you write to it you can only write one line at a time.

In any programming language you will need to follow these steps to access data in the text file:

1. Tell the program where the file is

2. Open the file to read from it (opens the file with a pointer pointing to the first line)

3. Read a line/lines of text from the file (this will automatically move the pointer down to the next line)

4. Close the file

Writing to the file follows the same idea:

1. Open the file to write to

2. To add/append to the file the pointer must be pointing at the end of the file (read lines until End of File, and then write the new one)

3. Remember to close the file at the end

Example 15: Writing to a file

In this example we will ask the user to input a list of names, and write them in a text file.

```
namefile = openwrite("names.txt")
while name != "xxx"
   name = input("Please enter name: ")
   namefile.writeline(name)
endwhile
namefile.close
```

In this version of the program, the dummy record "xxx" will be written to the file. If you don't want that to happen, you need to arrange for the read statement to be the last statement in the loop, so that the loop condition is tested immediately after reading.

```
namefile = openwrite("names.txt")
name = input("Please enter name: ")
while name != "xxx"
   namefile.writeline(name)
   name = input("Please enter name: ")
endwhile
namefile.close
```

Example 16: Reading from a file

Now the names are stored on the file, we can read them back and print them out, or store them in an array where they could be sorted, for example. In this example, there is a "dummy" name at the end of the file.

```
namefile = openread("names.txt")
name = namefile.readline()
while name != "xxx"
    print(name)
    name = namefile.readline()
endwhile
namefile.close
```

Example 17: Reading records into an array

In this example, we will assume that the file of names has exactly 10 records.

```
array names[10]
namefile = openread("names.txt")
for n = 0 to 9
    names[n] = namefile.readline()
next n
```

 Q23 Write pseudocode for a procedure which allows the user to input the daily maximum temperatures for a week, and write them to a text file.

Comma-separated value (.csv) files

Text files can contain more complex data and sometimes you will see **comma separated value** files that attempt to structure the line of text into fields, a bit like fields in a record of a database. The filename will have the suffix **.csv** but it is still essentially a text file. You still have lines of text, the only difference is that commas separate each field. Some programs will recognise this format and interpret it as separate data items on a line. Spreadsheets will do this. Here is a csv file with more students' scores in it

You can process the csv file in exactly the same way as a text file. Use string handling commands to find the commas and the text between commas.

Ch 1 scores - Notepad

File Edit Format View Help

```
Fred,23,24,27,24
Sally,34,27,30,31
Jimmy,29,30,28,34
Deborah,27,27,26,30
Cynthia,32,35,30,31
Dev,30,25,32,30
Adie,24,17,23,27
```

Viewed in notepad, as a text file

	A	B	C	D	E	F
1	Fred	23	24	27	24	
2	Sally	34	27	30	31	
3	Jimmy	29	30	28	34	
4	Deborah	27	27	26	30	
5	Cynthia	32	35	30	31	
6	Dev	30	25	32	30	
7	Adie	24	17	23	27	
8						

How it looks if you open it in Excel

Exercises

1. Julie is writing a computer game that simulates a 100m race. Each time the space bar is pressed, the position of the player moves up by 1. When the position reaches 100, the player has won.

    Here is Julie's algorithm for the program.

    ```
    CONST PlayerKey = " "
    Position = 0
    REPEAT
        INPUT KeyPressed
        IF KeyPressed = PlayerKey THEN
                Position = Position + 1
        END IF
    UNTIL Position = 100
    ```

    (a) State an example of a constant and a variable in the algorithm above. [2]

    (b) State what is meant by selection and iteration using examples from Julie's algorithm. [4]

    (c) To make the game more interesting, Julie changes the rules. Each time the spacebar is pressed, the position of the player will now move up by a random number.

    State **two** changes that need to be made to include this new rule.
    Justify each change. [4]

    OCR A451/01 June 2013 Qu 7

2. A mail-order company buys dresses from America and France to sell in the UK.

    The company uses the following algorithm to convert sizes before printing them in its catalogue. Half sizes are not possible (e.g. size 12.5).

    ```
    INPUT Size
    INPUT Origin
    IF Origin = "America" THEN
        Size = Size + 2
    ELSE
        IF Origin = "France" THEN
                Size = Size - 26
        END IF
    END IF
    PRINT Size
    ```

    (a) The code uses the variables `Origin` and `Size`.

    (i) Describe what is meant by a variable. [2]

    (ii) State the most appropriate data type for the variables `Origin` and `Size`, giving a reason for your choice.

    `Origin` [2]

    `Size` [2]

(b) The company sells the following dresses.

Dress A	**Dress B**	**Dress C**
Origin: France	Origin: America	Origin: UK
Size: 40	Size: 8	Size: 12

(c) State the size which will be printed in the catalogue using the algorithm given, for each of Dress A, Dress B and Dress C. [3]

OCR A451/01 Jan 2012 Qu 3

3. Santos is writing a program that guesses the number of goals a team will score in a football match. The algorithm for his program is shown below:

```
1   CONST Noise = 10
2   INPUT Wins
3   INPUT Losses
4   Goals = 0
5   Net = Wins - Losses
6   WHILE Net > Noise
7   Goals = Goals + 1
8   Net = Net - Noise
9   END WHILE
10  OUTPUT Goals
```

(a) State what is meant by a constant and give an example from the algorithm above. [2]

(b) State what is meant by a variable and give an example from the algorithm above. [2]

(c) State the number of goals that will be output by this algorithm for the following inputs. Explain how you obtained your answer in each case.

Wins = 30   Losses = 25 [3]

OCR A451/01 Jun 2014 Qu 10

4. A taxi uses a computer to communicate with central office and to calculate customers' fares.

(a) The program in the computer uses sequence, selection and iteration. State whether the operations below use **sequence**, **selection** or **iteration**.

(i) Performing a series of different set-up operations when the computer is switched on.

(ii) Beeping repeatedly after a message is sent, until the driver presses a button to show that the message has been read.

(iii) Deciding whether to use the `DayTimeRate` or the `EveningRate` functions to calculate a customer's fare. [3]

(b) The computer measures the distance travelled as a real number and then rounds it up to the next integer.

State what is meant by

(i) a real number [1]

(ii) an integer [1]

(c)   The cost of a day-time journey is £3 for the first kilometre and £2 for every kilometre after that. If there are five or more passengers in the taxi, an extra 50% is added to the charge.

Write an algorithm to calculate the cost of a day-time journey. Your algorithm should:

• allow the number of passengers and the distance of the journey to be input as whole numbers

• calculate the cost of the journey

• output the cost that has been calculated.   [7]

OCR A451 June 2012 Qu 12

5.   A file contains the following records:

ProductCode	ProductName	Price	QtyInStock	OnOrder
T4578	Baked beans	0.50	288	N
T5632	Tomato soup	0.63	170	N
D1144	Butter	1.56	17	Y
B8443	Tea bags	1.75	580	N
B7761	Instant coffee	2.56	22	N
D5229	Greek yoghurt	0.85	28	Y
D1258	Pizza	1.25	57	N

(a)   What data type would be suitable for each field in the records?   [5]

(b)   Write SQL statements to find the following:

(i)   The product code, product name, quantity in stock of all products which are on order.   [3]

(ii)   Product code, product name and quantity in stock of all products where the product code begins with the letter "D" and the quantity in stock is less than 30.   [3]

(iii)   Product name and code of all products priced between 60p and £2.00.   [3]

6.   (a)   The following pseudocode uses a function which accepts a time in hours, minutes and seconds and converts this to a number of seconds.

```
function timeInSeconds(hours, minutes, seconds)
    timeElapsed = (hours * 60 * 60) + (Minutes * 60) + seconds
    return timeElapsed
endfunction
```

Write one or more statements to call the function and print the number of seconds in 3:15:56, which is in the format hh:mm:ss.   [3]

(b)   Write a procedure which accepts a person's age as a parameter. If the age is less than 17, print out "You cannot hold a full driving licence". Otherwise, print out "You are eligible for a full driving licence."

Show how you would call the procedure.   [4]

7.   Write a pseudocode algorithm which simulates throwing a six-sided die 1000 times.
An array called face[1..6] is to hold the number of times each number (between 1 and 6) is thrown.

Print out the number of times each number is thrown.   [5]

Section 7

Logic and languages

Objectives

- Draw simple logic diagrams using the operations AND, OR and NOT

- Draw truth tables

- Apply logical operators in appropriate truth tables to solve problems

- Describe defensive design considerations:

  - o   input sanitisation/validation

  - o   planning for contingencies

  - o   anticipating misuse

  - o   authentication

- Use comments and indentation to assist maintainability of programs

- Understand the purpose of testing

- Describe types of testing: iterative and terminal

- Learn how to identify syntax and logic errors

- Select and use suitable test data

- Describe the characteristics and purpose of different levels of programming language, including low-level language

- Understand the purpose of translators

- Describe the characteristics of an assembler, a compiler and an interpreter

7

7.1 – Logic diagrams and truth tables

Binary Logic in programming

Understanding how binary logic works will help your programming. In your programs you often use complex Boolean expressions to control loops and selection statements – for example:

```
while NOT(EndOfFile) AND NOT (ItemFound)……

if (X <= 10) OR (CurrentCharNum > LengthOfString) then ……
```

You have probably programmed a `repeat` loop to carry on until the user typed an "N" or "n". The loop would look something like this with the condition at the end:

```
repeat
    |
    |
    |
until (response == 'N')  OR  (response == 'n')
```
             Boolean Expression   *Boolean Expression*

Each Boolean expression can be replaced with a letter which is called a **Boolean variable**.

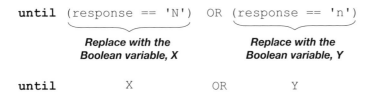

```
until (response == 'N')  OR  (response == 'n')
```
      Replace with the   **Replace with the**
      Boolean variable, X   **Boolean variable, Y**

```
until         X         OR         Y
```

Just like the Boolean data type in programming, Boolean variables are either **True** or **False**. X and Y will be either True or False. We equate True with 1 and False with 0 to represent electronic circuits being open or closed, just like with binary.

Circuit closed = 1 = True   Circuit open = 0 = False

Logic diagrams

Computers are based on electrical circuits where we can detect whether current is flowing or not. Binary uses base 2, so we have just two possible values 1 or 0. Representing data as binary values means we have to detect just two values in electrical circuits.

Binary logic is about these most basic circuits. Circuits in computers are made up of many logic gates but at this level we are looking at just three of them: **AND**, **OR** and **NOT**. A given input will generate an output based on the logic gate in use.

We use specific symbols to represent the different logic gates; these are standard symbols. They can be used to represent Boolean expressions such as Q = NOT A AND (B OR C).

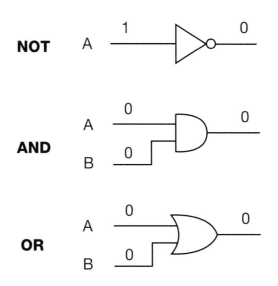

The logic gates can be joined up to make a circuit. For example NOT (A OR (B AND C)):

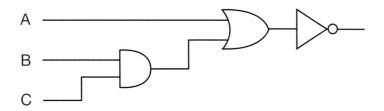

Logic gates and truth tables

Each of the AND, OR and NOT gates can be represented by a truth table showing the output, given each possible input or combination of inputs. Inputs are usually given algebraic letters such as A, B and C and output is usually represented by P or Q.

NOT gate

The NOT gate is represented by the symbol below and inverts the input. The small circle denotes an inverted input. If A is 1 (True), then NOT A is 0 (False).

Using 1s and 0s as inputs to a gate, its operation can summarised in the form of a **truth table**.

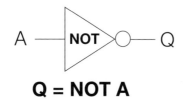

Q = NOT A

Input A	Output Q
0	1
1	0

The Boolean algebraic expression is written: $Q = \neg A$ where $\neg$ represents NOT.

AND gate

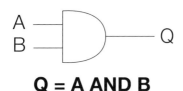

Q = A AND B

Input A	Input B	Output Q
0	0	0
0	1	0
1	0	0
1	1	1

The Boolean expression for AND is written: Q = A ∧ B where ∧ represents AND.

The truth table reflects the fundamental property of the AND gate: the output of A AND B is 1 (True) only if input A and input B are both 1 (True).

OR gate

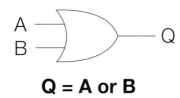

Q = A or B

Input A	Input B	Output Q
0	0	0
0	1	1
1	0	1
1	1	1

The Boolean expression for OR is written: Q = A ∨ B where ∨ represents OR.

If A = 0 (False) and B = 0 (False) then A OR B = 0 (False), otherwise A OR B = 1 (True).

7 Combining logic gates into logic circuits

These logic gates can be combined to form more complex logic circuits which can carry out a number of functions. They are the basic building blocks of many electronic circuits found in computer memories, household devices, computer management systems in cars, and so on. Look at the logic circuit below and follow the accompanying truth table.

Example 1

The logic circuit below represents the Boolean condition (NOT A AND B) OR (A AND C)

This can be written (¬A ∧ B) ∨ (A ∧ C)

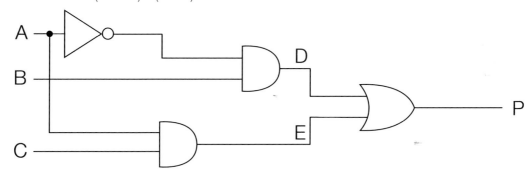

The truth table representing the above logic circuit:

A	B	C	NOT A	D = ¬A ∧ B	E = A ∧ C	P = D ∨ E
0	0	0	1	0	0	0
0	0	1	1	0	0	0
0	1	0	1	1	0	1
0	1	1	1	1	0	1
1	0	0	0	0	0	0
1	0	1	0	0	1	1
1	1	0	0	0	0	0
1	1	1	0	0	1	1

Q1 Write the expression representing the logic circuit below, and complete the truth table

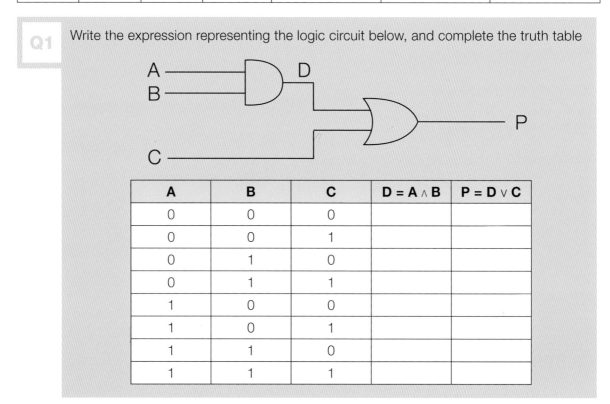

A	B	C	D = A ∧ B	P = D ∨ C
0	0	0		
0	0	1		
0	1	0		
0	1	1		
1	0	0		
1	0	1		
1	1	0		
1	1	1		

7.2 – Defensive design

Validating input data

Most programs require input from a user and so, in order to make sure the program will not crash or do something unexpected if the user enters something wrongly, all input data must be checked as soon as it is input. Several types of **validation check** can be carried out:

- **Range check:** a number or date is within a sensible/allowed range
- **Type check:** data is the right type such as an integer or a letter or text
- **Length check:** text entered is not too long or too short – for example, a password is greater than 8 characters, a product description is no longer than 25 characters
- **Presence check:** checks that data has been entered, i.e. that a field has not been left blank
- **Format check:** checks the format of, for example, a postcode or email address is appropriate

Validation can only check if a data item is reasonable. It cannot tell if it is correct. This is an important differentiation. If the "Student's Details" form prompts for **Date of Birth** the application can check that the data entered would be appropriate for that age group, but it cannot tell if you entered November instead of December by mistake.

Whilst validation ensures that the data entered are sensible, **verification** double-checks that it has been typed in correctly. Data is entered twice and the two versions are compared. If they are different the user can be prompted to try again. This is commonly used where email addresses and passwords are entered on forms.

Example 2

The following algorithm asks the user to enter their name and age. The name must be between 2 and 20 characters,

```
name = input("Please enter name: ")
while (name.length < 2) OR (name.length > 20)
   print("Must be between 2 and 20 characters – please re-enter: ")
   name = input("Please enter name: ")
endwhile
```

Example 3

The following algorithm asks the user to enter an integer between 17 and 30, and validates it. The number is then multiplied by 3 and the result printed out.

```
num = input("Enter number between 17 and 30: ")
while num < "17" OR num > "30"
   num = input ("invalid number – please re-enter: ")
endwhile
number = int(num)
print(number * 3)
```

Note that `num` has to be entered as a string in case the user enters a non-numeric character, which would cause the program to crash when the multiplication is performed.

Maintainability

There are several ways in which you can help to make your program code understandable.

- Use comments to say what the purpose of the program is, who wrote the program and when
- Use comments to explain how any difficult bit of code works, or what particular variables are used for
- Split the program into subroutines which each perform a single well-defined task
- Include comments with each subroutine to describe its purpose
- Use indentation so that it is clear where iteration and selection statements end. Some languages such as Python will give a syntax error if the indentation is not correct
- Use meaningful variable names for all variables
- Use constants for values such as VAT rate or π which will not change during execution of a program
- Aim for clarity rather than 'clever code' which is difficult for someone else to understand

All these techniques will help you when you return to a program after a few months and cannot remember what it is about or how it works.

Authentication routines

Authentication of an individual is used to make sure that a person is who they say they are. Methods could include optical, facial or fingerprint recognition.

A simple identification routine is used when you log into a school network, or an online shopping site. Usually, you will be assigned a user ID and you choose a password when you first log in. The password is encrypted and saved in a file. When you enter your user ID the password is looked up and compared to the one stored.

> **Q2** Why are you normally only allowed three attempts to type in the correct password?

Planning for contingencies

In Section 6.3, Example 5 you saw a simple routine to check a user password, giving them three attempts to get it right.

Example 4

Example 4 shows a **verification** check, in which a new user logging on to a website for the first time chooses a password, and then has to re-enter it to make sure they typed in what they intended.

```
password = input("Please enter password: ")
storedPassword = password
password = input("Confirm password: ")
if password == storedPassword then
   print ("Password accepted")
else
   print ("Invalid - Passwords don't match")
endif
```

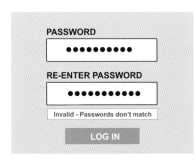

> **Q3** Can you think of any other checks that should be made on a user password before it is accepted?
>
> Amend the routine so that the user can start again if their password is rejected.

Data sanitisation routines

This is the process of making sensitive information safe for anyone to see. A simple example is displaying asterisks or dots when a password is typed in, so that no one can see what was typed as in Example 4.

It also includes measures taken to prevent unauthorised users from hacking into personal or company information – for example, bank account details. Various measures can be put in place such as:

- user access rights
- passwords
- encryption of sensitive data
- masking data

Masking data is often used when entering passwords or when an online shopping site requests debit or credit card details. The card number you gave last time you shopped is displayed, but with the middle 8 digits replaced by xxxx xxxx. Alternatively, only the last 4 digits may be displayed:

7.3 – Errors and testing

When you write a program in a high-level programming language, a translator (compiler or interpreter, see Section 7.4) will scan each line of code and convert it into machine code. As you will already have found out, programming is not as easy as it looks!

- Firstly, it is very easy to make mistakes typing in the code, for example typing "`prnt`" instead of "`print`". These are syntax errors.
- Secondly, once you have corrected all the syntax errors, the code may run but not do what you want. This means there are logic errors in your program.

Syntax errors

The translator expects commands to have a certain format, called syntax, just like a sentence in English has grammar rules. Syntax is a set of rules which defines the format of each command.

For example, in Visual Basic an if statement must have this format:

```
If x = 10 Then
    grade = "Pass"
Else
    grade = "Fail"
End If
```

In Python, the format of an **if** statement is written slightly differently:

```
If x == 10:
    grade = "Pass"
Else
    grade = "Fail"
```

Q4 If you put end if at the end of the if statement in Python, you will see a message similar to the one below when you try to execute the code. How else does the syntax of the if statement differ from that of Visual Basic?

```
"generation.py", line 18
        endif
           ^
SyntaxError: Invalid syntax
```

Without the correct key words the compiler will not be able to translate it into machine code and will give a syntax error.

Some common syntax errors include:

- mistyping a key word: `WRIET` instead of `WRITE`
- missing key words out of constructs such as starting a `repeat` loop but not writing `until` anywhere
- opening brackets but not closing them
- not having the right number of parameters inside brackets for functions, for example:

  ```
  answer = round(theNumber)
  ```

  will give a syntax error if the language expects another parameter to state the number of decimal places:

  ```
  answer = round(theNumber,2)
  ```

A program will not compile or run if there are syntax errors.

Logic errors

Once the code is written correctly, with no syntax errors, the program will compile. It can then be run – but just because it runs, that does not mean it is working correctly. Often when the program is run it doesn't do quite what was expected. This is called a **logic error.**

Typical logic errors that you have probably coded already include:

- Missing brackets from mathematical calculations:

  ```
  NetPay = GrossPay - TaxFreePart * TaxRate
  ```

  is not the same as:

  ```
  NetPay =(GrossPay - TaxFreePart) * TaxRate
  ```

- Loops that do not execute the correct number of times because a condition is written wrongly, e.g.

  `x > 10` instead of `x >= 10`

- Variables that have not been initialised, or have been initialised in the wrong place (often incorrectly initialised inside the loop instead of just before it)
- Flawed algorithms that just don't do what they were intended to do. Capturing all of the complexities of real-life scenarios in code is difficult and users often manage to do something to the input that you didn't cater for!

Often these logic errors are hard to spot. You should always do a visual check of output to check it isn't ridiculous but you also need to do some systematic testing to make sure the program really does behave as expected.

> **Q5** The flow diagram below does not produce correct results.
>
> Study it and state the likely purpose of the algorithm. Find the error(s) in the flow diagram and produce a corrected version. Explain what the errors are in the original attempt.

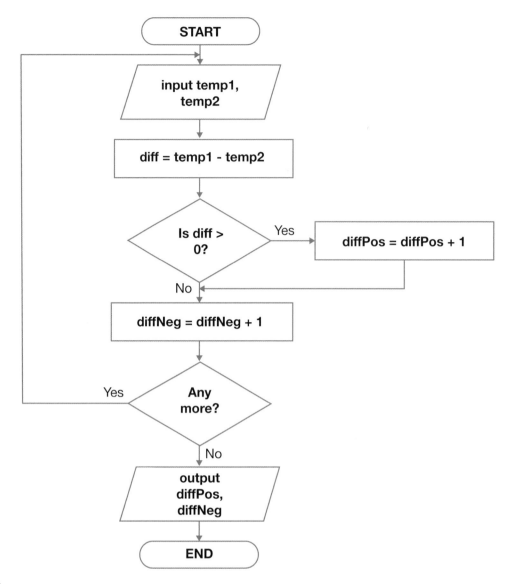

Testing

How do you know if your program really works? It may run and produce output but you need to check that the output is as expected. If you made a spreadsheet that multiplied pounds by a conversion rate to get dollars you would probably type in an easy number like £10 to see if the number of dollars looked right. We test programs in a similar way. We decide on some sensible test values to put into the program to test that the outputs are what we expect.

Planning how to test a program

A good way of planning your testing is to write down what sample data you will use to make sure the program works correctly, whatever the input. This is a **test plan**. It is important that you think about this before you write the program so you don't move the goalposts later. Remember, the aim of testing is to try and identify, for example, errors in calculations or user input which the program cannot handle, not to prove that the program usually works correctly.

You can formalise your plan by using a table with the following headings:

No.	Test purpose	Test data	Expected outcome	Actual outcome

The first three columns are part of the design and planning stage and the final column is completed when you test the finished program.

If numbers or dates are being entered by the user then you should use test data that checks normal (typical), boundary (extreme) and erroneous data. **Boundary data** includes both ends of the allowed range (e.g. 1-10) as well as data that should not be allowed, just outside this range.

✗	✓	✓	✗
0	1 to 10		11

Allowed range of input values

The test plan for testing this validation could look like this:

No.	Test purpose	Test data	Expected outcome
1	Check lowest valid number between 1 and 10	1 (lowest valid number)	Input is accepted
2	Check highest valid number between 1 and 10	10 (highest valid number)	Input is accepted
3	Check invalid boundary data outside lower limit	0 (not allowed)	Error message is displayed and user is asked to enter number again
4	Check invalid boundary data outside upper limit	11 (not allowed)	Error message is displayed and user is asked to enter number again
5	Check valid entry between 1 and 10	5 (typical number)	Input is accepted
6	Check invalid non-numeric entry	? (non-numerical entries not allowed)	Error message is displayed and user is asked to enter number again

If text is being entered, check what happens when you enter nothing or a string that is too long, as well as the text you would expect to be accepted.

No.	Test purpose	Test data	Expected outcome
7	Check that a correct password works	"frogs" (correct password)	User allowed to continue
8	Check that an error message is displayed when an incorrect password is entered	"cats" (incorrect password)	Error message is displayed and user is asked to enter password again
9	Check that an error message is displayed when an empty string is entered	"" (no password)	Error message is displayed and user is asked to enter password again

Using a trace table

A trace table is a standard tool for tracking how the value of each variable changes as you go through your algorithm line by line.

Example 5

The algorithm is designed to work out the average of test scores for a class of 10 students. The scores have already been input into an array called "scores". The average should be the sum of the scores divided by the number of scores. Here is the algorithm:

```
count = 0
totalScore = 0
repeat
    totalScore = totalScore + scores[count]
    count = count + 1
until count == 9
print(totalScore / 10)
```

Let's assume we have the following scores (out of 10) in the array:

Scores:

0	1	2	3	4	5	6	7	8	9
4	6	7	2	5	7	8	9	10	7

The total of these scores is 65. The average should be 65/10 = 6.5

The trace table for this algorithm looks like this:

scores(count)	totalScore	count	output
	0	0	
4	4	1	
6	10	2	
7	17	3	
2	19	4	
5	24	5	
7	31	6	
8	39	7	
9	48	8	
10	58	9	5.8

The total of these scores is 58. This makes the average 5.8

The trace tables show we exited the loop because `count = 9`, without processing the 10th result!

The algorithm needs adjusting so the loop says:

```
until count == 10 or until count > 9
```

Types of testing

Iterative testing is carried out using the test plan and trace tables, correcting the errors in a program and retesting until all tests give the expected result. Each subroutine may be tested separately in a large program, as soon as it is written.

Final or **terminal testing** will be carried out when the program is completely finished and all parts of it have been separately tested. The user will test the program to check that all the required functions have been included, everything works correctly whatever data is entered, and nothing is missing. You cannot test a module if it has not been written!

7.4 – Translators and facilities of languages

Classification of programming languages

Programming languages can be broadly divided into two categories:

- **low-level languages** (assembly languages and machine code) and
- **high-level languages** such as Python, Visual Basic, Delphi, Java and many others

The program code, once translated into binary, is referred to as **machine code**. To write code at the processor level we use **assembly language**. There are many different assembly languages; one for each different processor architecture. The code is written using **mnemonics**, abbreviated text commands such as LDA (LOAD), STO (STORE), ADD. Machine code is also processor-specific.

Human beings find it easier to write programs in languages that are suited to the type of problem they are trying to solve and that look more like normal languages, and **high-level languages** were invented for this. There are many different programming languages to suit different types of problem. For example, you might use Visual Basic to write a forms-based data processing application but you might use Java to code web-based applets.

Type of language	Example	Characteristics	Sample instructions
High-level language	Python, Visual Basic, Java, C++	Independent of hardware (portable) Translated using a compiler or interpreter One statement translates into many machine code instructions	rate = 3.02 used = 5672 billAmount = rate * used
Low-level language	Assembly language	Language is processor specific Translated using an assembler One statement translates into one machine code instruction	STO &39FC LDA #34 ADD &4F3A
	Machine code	Executable binary code produced by compiler, interpreter or assembler	1010100011010101 0100100101010101

Characteristics and use of programming languages

High-level languages such as Python and Visual Basic are relatively easy to learn and much faster to program in. Since statements written in these languages look a bit like English or maths, they are easier to read and understand, debug and maintain.

Specialised high-level languages have been developed to make the programming as quick and easy as possible for particular applications. SQL, for example, was specifically written to make it easy to search and maintain databases. HTML, CSS and JavaScript were developed to enable people to create web pages and websites.

Assembly language is often used in **embedded systems** such as the computer systems that control a washing machine, automobile or traffic lights. It has the following features which make it suitable for this type of application:

- It gives the programmer complete control over the system components so it can be used to **control and manipulate specific hardware components**
- Very efficient code can be written for a particular type of processor, so it will occupy **less memory** and **execute faster** than a compiled high-level language

Translating programs into machine code

Whatever language a program is written in, it must be translated into machine code so it can run on the processor. Translators are a type of **system software**. There are three types of translator program that do this.

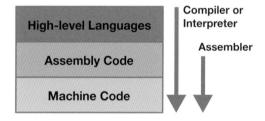

Assemblers

An **assembler** converts assembly language into machine code. This is a simple conversion as, in general, every assembly language instruction is translated into a single machine code instruction.

Compiler

A **compiler** translates a program written in a high-level programming language into machine code. This is a more complex translation as a single instruction can result in many machine code instructions. Different compilers for a particular language are needed for different types of processor.

The code written by the programmer is known as **source code**, and the machine code produced by the compiler is called object code. When you buy commercial software you are buying the **object code**, and you do not need the compiler in order to run the software.

For the developer, this has the advantage that someone buying the software cannot see the source code or copy it.

Interpreter

An **interpreter** is also used to translate high-level language code into machine code. Unlike a compiler, it translates each line of source code and then executes it, and no object code is produced. You have to have the interpreter installed on your computer in order to run the software.

The interpreter is often used when software is being developed as it is easy to pinpoint where there is an error in the code. The program will run up to the point where the interpreter finds a syntax error and then stop and highlight the error.

A long, complex program will take considerably more time to execute if it is being interpreted. For example, if a loop is performed 10,000 times, the lines within the loop are translated 10,000 times.

The distinction between a compiler and an interpreter is not completely clear-cut, however. Some languages such as JavaScript, which is used in creating web pages, are compiled into an intermediate stage called bytecode. This can be interpreted and run on many different types of processor using an appropriate bytecode interpreter, so that the web page can be viewed on any type of computer.

The table below compares compilers and interpreters:

Compiler	Interpreter
Translates the whole program to produce the executable object code	Translates and executes one line at a time
Compiled program executes faster as it is already in machine code	Interpreted programs take more time to execute because each instruction is translated before it is executed
Customers do not need to have the compiler installed on their computer to run the software	Customers must have the interpreter installed on their computer
Customers cannot see the actual source code when you distribute the program	Customers can see the source code and could copy it
Used for software that will be run frequently or copyright software sold to a third party	Used for program development and to interpret bytecode

Facilities of an IDE

When you create a program you will be using a software package that helps you write the code more easily.

This is called an **Integrated Development Environment** or **IDE**.

The screenshot below shows the Komodo IDE which can be used to enter, compile and run Python programs.

The IDE provides the many tools to help you enter, edit, compile, test and debug your programs.

> **Q6** Describe the facilities of an IDE that you have used, which help you to write clear, maintainable code, find logic errors in your code, or provide other useful features.

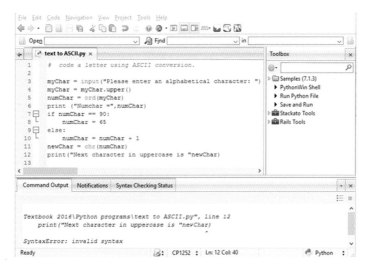

Entering a new program

In the screenshot above, you can see a menu at the top of the screen. Choosing **File, New** will present you with a blank screen to **type** your program.

The program is typed in the main window. Python adds line numbers for easy reference. You can save it using an option from the File menu. You can also **edit** your code.

Compiling and running your program

When you are ready to try out your program, it first has to be translated into machine code. This will be done using a **compiler** or **interpreter**.

Double-clicking the option **Save and Run** in the **Toolbox** on the right of the window will **translate** the program and report any **syntax errors**.

In the window below, the compiler has found a syntax error, and it tells you what line the error is on. A comma is missing, so you can correct the program and double-click Save and Run again. This time, the program runs and the output is displayed in the bottom window.

Programming in interactive mode

Another very useful facilities of some IDEs is being able to try out bits of code in **Interactive**

Mode. Selecting PythonWin Shell from the Toolbox on the right brings up the Interactive window, in which Python will immediately translate and run any statement you type. If it doesn't understand the statement, it outputs nothing and you know you've got it wrong!

Many other options are available in any IDE. You need to experiment with the IDE that you use to find out some of the other useful things it will do for you.

Exercises

1. The following logic diagram shows the expression NOT (A AND B)

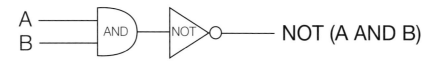

Complete the missing boxes in the truth table below to show the value of NOT (A AND B) that will be output for each possible set of values of a and b.

A	B	NOT (A AND B)
0	0	1
0		1
1	0	

[4]

OCR A451/01 June 2014 Qu 7

2. (a) State the output of each of the following logic circuits for the inputs given. [2]

(b) Fig. 1 is a circuit diagram.

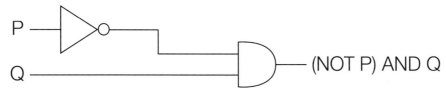

Complete the truth table for Fig. 1.

P	Q	(NOT P) AND Q
0	0	0
1	0	0

[3]

OCR A451/01 Jan 2013 Qu 3

3. Charley is writing a program for music students. To make sure that there are no logic errors in the program, Charley uses a test plan.

   (a) Describe what is meant by a logic error. [2]

   (b) The program uses the letters in the following list to represent musical notes.

   C D E F G A B

   When the user inputs a letter from this list, the program outputs the next three notes in the list. If it gets to the end of the list, it starts again from the beginning, so the next note after B is C.

Complete the test plan below by stating, for each input data, the expected outcome and a reason for the test.

Input Data	Expected outcome	Reason for test
C		
A		
H		

[6]

OCR A451/01 Jan 2013 Qu 9

4. Jim is writing a program to calculate the wages of workers in a teddy bear factory.

   (a) Jim uses an Integrated Development Environment (IDE) to create the program.

   Describe **two** tools in an IDE that can help Jim when creating the program. [4]

   (b) Workers sometimes get a £50 bonus.

   Here is the algorithm used to calculate whether a worker should get a bonus.

   ```
   Limit = 200
   INPUT WagesEarned
   IF WagesEarned < Limit THEN
        Pay = WagesEarned
   ELSE
        Pay = WagesEarned + 50
   END IF
   ```

   State the value of Pay after this code is executed for each of the following values of WagesEarned.

   WagesEarned = 50

   WagesEarned = 200 [2]

   (c) The wages earned by a worker is either £2 for every teddy bear they have made or £5 for every hour they have worked, whichever is larger.

   Write an algorithm that:

   • allows the user to input the number of teddy bears made and the number of hours worked

   • calculates the wages for the number of teddy bears made

   • calculates the wages for the number of hours worked

   • outputs the larger of the two results [6]

OCR A451/01 Jan 2013 Qu 12

5. A games developer is developing an online game that can be played on games consoles, desktop computers or mobile phones.

   (a) The program is written in high-level language and then translated to machine code.

   Describe **two** differences between high-level code and machine code. [4]

   (b) One type of translator which can be used is an interpreter.

   (i) Describe how an interpreter translates the high-level code to machine code. [2]

   (ii) State the name of a **different type** of translator, other than an interpreter, which can be used to translate high-level code to machine code. [1]

OCR A451/01 June 2012 Qu 11

Section 8

Data representation

Objectives

- Use the units bit, nibble, byte, kilobyte, megabyte, gigabyte, terabyte and petabyte

- Understand how data need to be converted into a binary format to be processed by a computer

- Convert positive denary whole numbers (0-255) into 8-bit binary numbers and vice-versa

- Add two positive binary numbers and explain overflow errors which may occur

- Apply a binary shift and understand its effect

- Convert positive denary whole numbers (0-255) into 2-digit hexadecimal numbers and vice-versa

- Convert from binary to hexadecimal equivalents and vice versa

- Understand the use and function of check digits

- Explain the use of binary codes to represent characters

- Explain the term "character set" and the relationship between the number of bits per character in a character set and the number of characters which can be represented (for example ASCII, extended ASCII and Unicode)

- Explain how an image is represented as a series of pixels represented in binary

- Describe the metadata included in the file

- Describe the effect of colour depth and resolution on the size of an image file

- Explain how sound can be sampled and stored in digital form

- Explain how sampling intervals and other factors affect the size of a sound file and the quality of its playback:
  - sample size
  - bit rate
  - sampling frequency

- Explain the need for compression

- Explain types of compression: lossy and lossless

8

8.1 – Storage units and binary numbers

Computers are made up of complicated hardware that stores and processes data. If you break a computer down into its most basic components you have millions of circuits that either allow electricity to flow, or not. Imagine a whole row of light switches that you can switch on and off in different combinations to mean different things. Each switch is either on or off. It has only two states, which can be represented by 1 or 0. This is called **binary**.

A single **1** or **0** is a binary digit, or a **bit** for short. A group of eight bits is called a **byte**.

Imagine you've taken a small bite out of an apple, you might call that a nibble. So four bits, half a byte, is called a **nibble**.

Units

The byte is the smallest adressable unit of memory in a computer. Just as a kilometer is 1000 meters, we can group together 1000 bytes to make a **kilobyte**.

Memory size is measured in the following multiples:

Unit	Number of bytes	Equivalent denary value	
Kilobyte (KB)	10^3	1,000	bytes
Megabyte (MB)	10^6	1,000,000	bytes
Gigabyte (GB)	10^9	1,000,000,000	bytes
Terabyte (TB)	10^{12}	1,000,000,000,000	bytes
Petabyte (PB)	10^{15}	1,000,000,000,000,000	bytes

(**Note:** 1MB = 1000KB etc. Internal memory often uses the kibibyte, where 1KiB (Kibibyte) = 2^{10} = 1,024 bytes, 1MiB (Mebibyte) = 2^{20} = 1,048,576 bytes, and so on).

Q1
(a) How many bytes in 1,000 Petabytes?
(b) Convert 4800MB into GB
(c) Convert 800TB into GB

Q2
(a) How big is a typical photograph file taken from a mobile phone camera?
(b) What is the average capacity of a hard disk or SSD on a computer?

Computers use the binary system to store numbers and perform binary arithmetic and logic operations. Computer systems have got larger and larger, and now the capacity of secondary storage systems is commonly measured in terabytes (TB). Vast computers used in universities and industrial applications have storage which is now measured in petabytes. Scientists have estimated that the human brain has a memory capacity of 2.5 petabytes so computers seem to be catching up!

Binary to denary conversion

Binary data uses only two digits, 0 and 1. Our denary system uses ten digits, 0 to 9.
The number 75, for example, is 7 tens plus 5 units.

Imagine you are back in primary school, learning to add again. 7 + 5 = 12, so you write down the 2 units but carry the group of 10.

23 would be 2 groups of 10 and 3 units.

Counting in binary

Counting in binary is the same except instead of digits 0 to 9 we only have two digits, 0 and 1, so we carry the group of 2. This is known as base 2 or binary. This is how we count to 10 in binary:

Denary	Binary	
0	0	
1	1	
2	10	Notice that we now go to the second column – one group of 2, no units
3	11	One group of 2 plus one unit 2 + 1 = 3
4	100	Now we go to the third column, 2 groups of previous column, so this is 4
5	101	
6	110	
7	111	
8	1000	Every time we go to the next column it is two times the previous column
9	1001	
10	1010	

Can you see the pattern? The column headings in a binary number double each time:

| | x 2 | | x 2 | | x 2 | | x 2 | | x 2 | | x 2 | | x 2 | |

128	64	32	16	8	4	2	1
2x2x2x2x2x2x2	2x2x2x2x2x2	2x2x2x2x2	2x2x2x2	2x2x2	2x2	2	1
2^7	2^6	2^5	2^4	2^3	2^2	2^1	2^0

Q3 Looking at the table above, what is 2^8?

Storing larger numbers

In order to store larger numbers, computers group 2, 4, 8 or more bytes into units called **words**. On this course you will be dealing only with binary numbers held in a single 8-bit byte.

Denary to binary conversion

To convert a denary number to a binary number, use the column headings. You need to find the highest column heading that you can take away from the number and start there:

To convert the denary number **57** into binary:

The highest column heading we can take out of 57 is 32 (the next one is 64, which is too high).

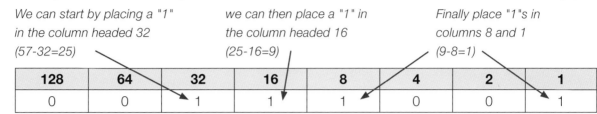

We can start by placing a "1"
in the column headed 32
(57-32=25)

we can then place a "1" in
the column headed 16
(25-16=9)

Finally place "1"s in
columns 8 and 1
(9-8=1)

128	64	32	16	8	4	2	1
0	0	1	1	1	0	0	1

Here are some more examples:

Denary	Binary							
	128	64	32	16	8	4	2	1
23 →	0	0	0	1	0	1	1	1
84 →	0	1	0	1	0	1	0	0
255 →	1	1	1	1	1	1	1	1

Each binary digit is called a **bit**. A group of eight bits is called a **byte**. You will notice in the examples above that we always write the binary numbers using eight bits. This is common practice. It is not incorrect to write the first binary value as 1 0 1 1 1 rather than 0 0 0 1 0 1 1 1 (without the leading zeros) but the second example is more commonly used.

> **Q4** Convert the following denary numbers into binary.
> (a) 19   (b) 63   (c) 142

Binary to denary conversion

To convert a binary number into denary, we add up the column values where a "1" appears. For example, to convert the binary number 01101100 to denary, write each number under a column heading, starting on the right with the least significant digit:

128	64	32	16	8	4	2	1
0	1	1	0	1	1	0	0

gives the value: **64** + **32** + **8** + **4 = 108**

More examples:

Denary	Binary							
	128	64	32	16	8	4	2	1
126 ←	0	1	1	1	1	1	1	0
213 ←	1	1	0	1	0	1	0	1
254 ←	1	1	1	1	1	1	1	0

> **Q5** Convert the following binary numbers into denary.
> (a) 00010111   (b) 10010110   (c) 11111111

8.2 – Binary arithmetic and hexadecimal

Addition of binary numbers

Adding binary works in exactly the same way as adding denary numbers except this time you carry groups of 2 instead of groups of 10:

Adding in denary	Adding in binary

1 2 3 4 5
    1 3 4 +
—————
1 2 4 7 9
	1 0 0 1 0
	    1 0 1 +
	—————
	1 0 1 1 1

7 8 2 3 5
     ₁9₁7 +
—————
7 8 3 3 2
	1 0 0 1 1
	     ₁1₁1₁1 +
	—————
	1 1 0 1 0

Notice that you carry 1 when you get to ten in a column so 5+7=12, write 2 in that column but carry one group of ten.	Notice that you carry 1 when you get to two in a column, so 1+1=2, write 0 in that column but carry one group of two. In the second column, 1+1+1=3, carry one group of 2 to the third column.

Some more examples:

```
10101100      00101101      00101101
00010001+     10000101+     10000111+
————————      ————————      ————————
10111101      10110010      10110100
```

Q6 Carry out the following binary number additions:

(a) 00110011 + 01000110

(b) 00010110 + 01110110

(c) 00001111 + 01110011

(d) 00101010 + 01111011

(e) 00011100 + 01110011

Overflow

The biggest number you can represent with 8 bits is 255 (i.e. 128+64+32+16+8+4+2+1).

If you add two binary numbers together that result in a number bigger than 255, it will need 9 bits. A computer stores things in memory in a finite amount of space. If you cannot represent the number in that amount of space because it is too big, then **overflow** occurs.

For example:

```
(252)  11111100
 (15)  00001111+
       ——————————
(267) 100001011
```

The computer would need 9 bits to represent 267 so this 9th bit doesn't fit in the byte allocated. This is what is meant by an **overflow** error.

Binary shifts

If a binary number is shifted to the left this is equivalent to multiplying the number by 2 for each shift to the left.

For example: If we shift

TWO places to the left we get the binary number:

(NOTE: Empty binary positions are filled with 0s as we shift to the left.)

The original binary number has a value of 15 (i.e. 1+2+4+8 = 15); the number after shifting two places to the left has the value 60 (i.e. 32+16+8+4 = 60). It is multiplied by 4, or 2^2.

Shifting binary numbers to the right has the opposite effect i.e. each shift to the right has the effect of dividing by 2. Thus if we shift

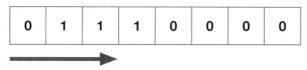

THREE places to the right we get the binary number:

The original binary value was 112 (i.e. 16+32+64 = 112) and the value after shifting three places to the right is 14 (i.e. 2+4+8 = 14). The number was divided by 8, or 2^3.

(NOTE: Empty binary positions are filled with 0s as we shift to the right.)

Multiplication/division by powers of 2

This gives an easy way to multiply and divide binary numbers by powers of 2.

- Shifting right one place divides the number by 2
- Shifting left one place multiplies the number by 2

This is equivalent to shifting a decimal number right or left – for example shifting 12300 right gives 1230, i.e. it divides the number by 10. Shifting left multiplies a decimal number by 10.

> **Q7** Write down the results after the following shift operations and write down the denary values before and after the shifts:
>
> (a) The number `11001100` is shifted TWO places to the right
>
> (b) The number `00011001` is shifted TWO places to the left
>
> (c) The number `11001000` is shifted THREE places to the right
>
> (d) The number `00000111` is shifted FOUR places to the left
>
> (e) The number `10000000` is shifted FIVE places to the right

Hexadecimal number system

Which of these is easier to remember: **01011011** or **5B**? Humans are not very good at remembering long strings of numbers so, to make it easier, we can represent every group of 4 bits (known as a **nibble**) with a single digit.

The smallest value you can hold in 4 bits is 0000. The largest value is 1111. This means that we need to represent the denary values 0 to 15 with a single digit. The trouble is, we only have numerical digits 0 to 9, so to get around this problem we use letters A to F to represent the digits 10, 11, 12, 13, 14 and 15.

This is called base 16 or, more commonly, **hexadecimal**. It is often abbreviated to **hex**.

Denary	Binary	Hex
0	0000	0
1	0001	1
2	0010	2
3	0011	3
4	0100	4
5	0101	5
6	0110	6
7	0111	7
8	1000	8
9	1001	9
10	1010	A
11	1011	B
12	1100	C
13	1101	D
14	1110	E
15	1111	F
16	0001 0000	10
255	1111 1111	FF

> *A single hex digit replaces 4 bits 15 is the biggest number you can have with 4 bits so 16 is one group of 16 and no units (just like we did with binary)*
>
> *255 represents 15 groups of 16 + 15 units (15 x 16) + 15 = 240 + 15*

Converting a binary number to hexadecimal

In GCSE Computing you will only need to work with 8-bit binary numbers, which can be represented as two hex digits. The left-hand hex digit represents groups of 16, the right-hand hex digit represents the units.

The denary number 92 =   **0101**   **1100**   = **5C** in hex
                              5   **12**   *(12 is replaced by C – see table above)*

> **Q8** Convert the following numbers from binary to hex:
> (a) 00010111
> (b) 11111100
> (c) 001100101110
> (d) 1101110001111111

Converting a denary number to hexadecimal

To convert the denary number 182 into hex the first step is to work out how many groups of 16 there are in 182. Secondly work out how many units are left over.

182 / 16 = 11 remainder 6

11 is B in hex. 6 is just 6   so 182 denary = B6 hex

Alternatively, you can convert the denary to binary first and then convert the binary to hex.

> **Q9** Convert the following numbers from denary to hex:
> (a) 77   (b) 255   (c) 186   (d) 18

Converting hexadecimal to binary

Converting a hexadecimal number into binary is a simple matter of converting each hex digit into a group of 4 binary digits. For example, to convert the hex number **A7** to binary:

A   7

↓   ↓

1010   **0111**

Further examples: **B 5** is 1 0 1 1   0 1 0 1
                       F A is 1 1 1 1   1 0 1 0

> **Q10** Convert the following hexadecimal numbers into binary
> (a) E4   (b) 8A   (c) FF   (d) C1

Converting hexadecimal to denary

To convert a hexadecimal number into denary, multiply the heading values by the hex digit. For example, to convert the hex number **A7** to binary:

A   7   (remember column place
                           values are: **16** and **1**)
↓   ↓

(10 x 16)   +   **(7 x 1)**   = **167** (remember: A = 10)

Further examples: **7 F** is 112 + 15 = **1 2 7**

                       C D is 192 + 13 = **2 0 5**

> **Q11** Convert the following hexadecimal numbers into denary
> (a) 77   (b) AF   (c) 17   (d) 20

Uses of hexadecimal

As hexadecimal is so much easier to understand and remember than binary, it has several applications in computing. One application you are probably familiar with is picking colours for a graphic.

Hex numbers are also used in Assembly language instructions such as `ADD &4F3A`.

Check digits

A **check digit** is an additional digit at the end of a string of other numbers designed to check for mistakes in input or transmission. Printed books and other products have a unique ISBN (International Standard Book Number), a 13-digit number which includes the calculated check digit and is printed with the barcode. The first 12 digits are the unique item number, the 13th is the check digit. This can be calculated using the **Modulo 10** system.

ISBN 978-0956143051

9 780956 143051

For example, the ISBN or EAN of 978095614305 has a check digit of 1, calculated as follows:

ISBN	9	7	8	0	9	5	6	1	4	3	0	5	1
Weight	1	3	1	3	1	3	1	3	1	3	1	3	
Multiplication	9	21	8	0	9	15	6	3	4	9	0	15	
Addition	Add all the numbers												99
Remainder	Find the remainder when divided by 10												9
Subtraction	Subtract the result from 10												1

The ISBN digits are given weights of 1 and 3 alternatively. Each value is multiplied by its weight. The multiplied values are added together and divided by 10 to get a remainder of 9. The remainder is subtracted from 10 to give a check digit of 1. The published check digit is read by a barcode scanner, an algorithm to check the check digit is performed and if, as in this case, the digits match, the barcode is deemed, with almost 100% accuracy, to have been read accurately.

A similar system works with credit card numbers.

> **Q12** Use the Modulo 10 system to check the check digit on a product or book barcode.

Using check digits for parity

A **parity bit** is an additional bit that is used to check that the other bits transmitted are likely to be correct. Using 7-bit ASCII with an 8-bit system meant that there was an extra bit available. This was used as a parity bit.

Computers use either odd or even parity, and the parity bit is used to ensure that the total number of 1s in each byte, including the parity bit, equals an odd or even number. For example an R is represented by 1010010 in 7-bit ASCII:

0	1	0	1	0	0	1	0

Using odd parity, the parity bit above is the most significant bit, and becomes 0 to make the total number of 1s an odd number – in this case, 3. Using even parity, the parity bit would have been set to 1.

> **Q13** What would be the parity bit value for 0010110 using odd parity?

8.3 – ASCII and Unicode

Every time a character is typed on a keyboard a code number is transmitted to the computer. The code numbers are stored in binary. PCs sometimes use a **character set** called **ASCII**, American Standard Code for Information Interchange.

The table below shows a version of ASCII that uses 7 bits to code each character. The biggest number that can be held in seven bits is 1111111 in binary (127 in denary). Therefore 128 different characters can be represented in the ASCII character set (using codes 0 to 127).

7-bit ASCII Table

ASCII	DEC	Binary	ASCII	DEC	Binary	ASCII	DEC	Binary	ASCII	DEC	Binary
NULL	000	000 0000	space	032	010 0000	@	064	100 0000	`	096	110 0000
SOH	001	000 0001	!	033	010 0001	A	065	100 0001	a	097	110 0001
STX	002	000 0010	"	034	010 0010	B	066	100 0010	b	098	110 0010
ETX	003	000 0011	#	035	010 0011	C	067	100 0011	c	099	110 0011
EOT	004	000 0100	$	036	010 0100	D	068	100 0100	d	100	110 0100
ENQ	005	000 0101	%	037	010 0101	E	069	100 0101	e	101	110 0101
ACK	006	000 0110	&	038	010 0110	F	070	100 0110	f	102	110 0110
BEL	007	000 0111	'	039	010 0111	G	071	100 0111	g	103	110 0111
BS	008	000 1000	(	040	010 1000	H	072	100 1000	h	104	110 1000
HT	009	000 1001	)	041	010 1001	I	073	100 1001	i	105	110 1001
LF	010	000 1010	*	042	010 1010	J	074	100 1010	j	106	110 1010
VT	011	000 1011	+	043	010 1011	K	075	100 1011	k	107	110 1011
FF	012	000 1100	,	044	010 1100	L	076	100 1100	l	108	110 1100
CR	013	000 1101	-	045	010 1101	M	077	100 1101	m	109	110 1101
SO	014	000 1110	.	046	010 1110	N	078	100 1110	n	110	110 1110
SI	015	000 1111	/	047	010 1111	O	079	100 1111	o	111	110 1111
DLE	016	001 0000	0	048	011 0000	P	080	101 0000	p	112	111 0000
DC1	017	001 0001	1	049	011 0001	Q	081	101 0001	q	113	111 0001
DC2	018	001 0010	2	050	011 0010	R	082	101 0010	r	114	111 0010
DC3	019	001 0011	3	051	011 0011	S	083	101 0011	s	115	111 0011
DC4	020	001 0100	4	052	011 0100	T	084	101 0100	t	116	111 0100
NAK	021	001 0101	5	053	011 0101	U	085	101 0101	u	117	111 0101
SYN	022	001 0110	6	054	011 0110	V	086	101 0110	v	118	111 0110
ETB	023	001 0111	7	055	011 0111	W	087	101 0111	w	119	111 0111
CAN	024	001 1000	8	056	011 1000	X	088	101 1000	x	120	111 1000
EM	025	001 1001	9	057	011 1001	Y	089	101 1001	y	121	111 1001
SUB	026	001 1010	:	058	011 1010	Z	090	101 1010	z	122	111 1010
ESC	027	001 1011	;	059	011 1011	[	091	101 1011	{	123	111 1011
FS	028	001 1100	<	060	011 1100	\	092	101 1100	|	124	111 1100
GS	029	001 1101	=	061	011 1101	]	093	101 1101	}	125	111 1101
RS	030	001 1110	>	062	011 1110	^	094	101 1110	~	126	111 1110
US	031	001 1111	?	063	011 1111	_	095	101 1111	DEL	127	111 1111

Using the ASCII table in programming

The character codes are grouped and run in sequence; i.e. if 'A' is 65 then 'C' must be 67. The pattern applies to other groupings such as digits and lowercase letters, so you can say that since '7' is 55, '9' must be 57.

Also, '7' < '9' and 'a' > 'A'.

Notice that the ASCII code value for '5' (0011 0101) is different from the pure binary value for 5 (0000 0101). That's why you can't calculate with numbers which are input as strings.

Character sets

Extended ASCII code

The basic ASCII codes use 7 bits for each character (as shown in the table above). This gives a total of 128 (2^7) possible unique symbols. The **extended ASCII** character set uses 8 bits, which gives an additional 128 characters (i.e. 256 in total). The extra characters represent characters from foreign languages and special symbols such as é, ® or ½.

Unicode

Unicode is the new standard for representing the characters of all the languages of the world, including Chinese, Arabic, Japanese and Greek characters:

العربيّة, 汉语, תִיְרִבְע, ελληνικά

Unicode uses twice as many bits (i.e. 16 bits) per character as extended ASCII and can represent 2^{16} (65,536) unique characters.

> Using extended 8-bit ASCII, how many bytes would be required to store the phrase 'Computer Science'?

8.4 – Images

Images can be stored in different ways on a computer. A drawing that you create in PowerPoint is a **vector** graphic. It is made up of lines and shapes with specific properties such as line style, line colour, fill colour, start point and end point. The computer stores all of this data about each shape in binary.

When you take a photograph on a digital camera, the image is not made up of individual shapes. The picture somehow has to capture the continuously changing set of colours and shades that make up the real-life view. To store this type of image on a computer the image is broken down into very small elements called **pixels**. A pixel (short for picture element) is one specific colour. The whole image may be set to, for example, 600 pixels wide by 400 pixels high.

The **size** or **resolution** of an image is expressed directly as the width in pixels by height in pixels, e.g. 600 x 400.

If the size of a picture is increased, then more pixels will need to be stored. This increases the size of the image file. This is a **bitmap** image.

Colour depth

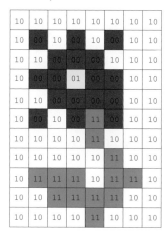

This image of a flower uses four colours. Therefore two bits are needed to record the colour of each pixel:

11	10	01	00

The number of bits used to store each pixel dictates how many colours an image can contain. 8 bits per pixel will give 256 possible colours. The number of bits per pixel is referred to as the **colour depth**. To work out the minimum required colour depth from the number of colours in the image, convert the number of colours to a power of 2.

For up to:

$2 = 2^1$ colours	1 bit is required per pixel
$4 = 2^2$ colours	2 bits are required
$8 = 2^3$ colours	3 bits are required
...	
$256 = 2^8$ colours	8 bits are required
$65,536 = 2^{16}$ colours	16 bits are required

If the **colour depth** is increased so more bits are used to represent each pixel, then the overall size of the file will increase.

If we record the value of each pixel in this image, starting from the top left-hand corner and going left to right across each row, we end up with the following data file:

```
10 10 10 10 10 10 10 10

10 00 10 00 10 00 10 10

10 10 00 00 00 10 10 10

10 00 00 01 00 00 10 10
```

etc.

Q15 Convert the following binary data into a 5 x 5 pixel image, where 1 represents black and 0 represents white:

```
1 1 1 1 1   0 0 1 0 0   0 0 1 0 0   0 0 1 0 0   0 0 1 0 0
```

The effect of colour depth and resolution

Colour depth is used to describe the maximum number of colours that can be used to represent an image. The higher the number of colours, the more faithful will be the image. This will clearly also affect the file size of the image.

We can have monochrome (black and white), grey scale (usually 256 shades of grey), 16-bit colour and 32-bit colour (known as true colour), for example.

2 colours   *4 colours*   *8 colours*   *16 colours*   *256 colours*   *65,536 colours* *16.7m colours*

The **resolution** of an image is the number of pixels (picture elements) or dots that make up an image. The greater the number of pixels, the sharper the image will be, and the larger the file size of the image. Pixel density, measured in pixels per inch (PPI), is used to describe the resolution of a computer screen, camera or scanner.

An image from the Internet is typically 72PPI, which is a low resolution. If you try to enlarge the image on the screen, the software makes up for the pixels which don't exist and you get a blurred image. The higher the resolution, the larger the image you can display on a screen without it looking blurred.

Example 1 Calculating the file size

An image captured in 256 colours, with a size of 2,100 pixels by 1,500 pixels, is saved on a memory stick. What is the size in bytes of the file?

Size in bytes = (image width x image height x colour depth) / 8

= (2,100 x 1,500 x 8) / 8 (256 colours = colour depth of 8 bits)

= 3,150,000 bytes (3.15MB)

> **Q16** Calculate the size in bytes of a black and white image that is 96 pixels wide and 1,024 pixels high.

> **Q17** Using a computer, try changing the resolution of an image to see how the sharpness and the size of the file change as the resolution is reduced.

8

Metadata

Metadata means "data about data". When a file is saved, information about the file is saved with it. This could include:

- Type of file
- Time and date of creation
- Creator or author of the data
- File size

This type of metadata can make it easier to find a particular file if you have forgotten the name you gave it, but can remember approximately when you created it.

Metadata about a digital image will also include:

- The dimensions of the image
- The image resolution
- The colour depth

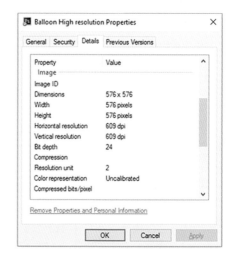

From this information, the computer can interpret the binary digits to recreate the image on screen or paper.

8.5 – Sound

Sound waves are **analogue**, which means continuously changing. Anything stored on a computer has to be stored in a **digital** format as a series of binary numbers. To store sound on a computer we need to convert the waveform into a numerical representation. The device that takes real-world analogue signals and converts them to a digital representation is called an **Analogue-to-Digital Converter** (**ADC**).

For sound waves, the analogue signal is converted as follows:

- Analogue sound is received by a microphone
- This is converted into an electrical analogue signal
- The signal amplitude (height of the wave) is measured at regular intervals (sampled)
- the values are rounded to a level (quantisation)
- the values are stored as a series of binary numbers

A **sample** is a measure of amplitude at a point in time. The accuracy with which an analogue sound wave is converted to a digital format depends on two things, **sample resolution** and **sample rate**.

The **sample resolution** is the number of bits used to store each sample. The two graphs below show how the amplitude of a wave is more accurately represented with a 4-bit sample resolution than with a 2-bit sample resolution.

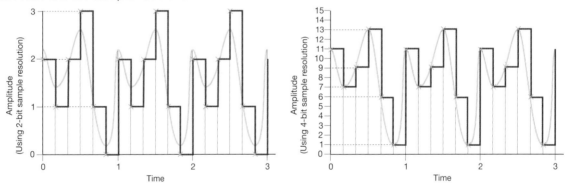

The **sample rate** is the frequency with which you record the amplitude of the sound, i.e. the number of samples per second. This is usually measured in Hertz, where 1 Hertz = 1 sample per second. The more frequently the sound is sampled, the better the quality of playback.

The more often you take a sample, the smoother the playback will sound. The two graphs below show how changing the sample rate increases or decreases the accuracy of the digital representation.

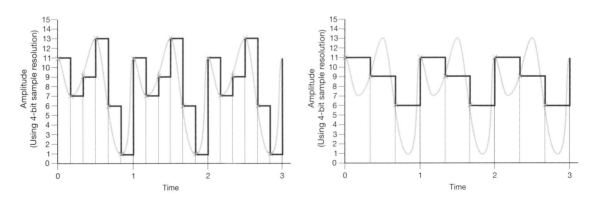

Factors affecting the size of a sound file and the quality of its playback

Sample rate: The number of samples taken in a second. This is usually measured in hertz, where

> 1 Hertz = 1 sample per second

The more frequently the sound is sampled, the better the quality of playback. In the graph above, samples are taken every 1 unit of time – if we halved the sample interval, the wave would be more accurately represented.

Sample resolution: The number of bits used to store each sample.

The more bits that are used, the better the accuracy of the recording. In the graph of a sound wave above, the sample resolution on the Y axis has 16 different amplitudes that a sample can be recorded at. It could be more accurately represented with 32 or more points, but this would increase the number of bits that must be stored for each sample.

Sample size: The number of seconds over which the sample was taken.

Example 2: Calculating the size of a sound file

The file size of a sound file = sample rate x sample resolution x seconds

A sample rate of 44.1kHz is typically used for CD audio, with a sample resolution of 16 bits per sample.

So the file size of a sample lasting 5 seconds would be

> (44.1 x 1000 x 16 x 5) / 8 bytes
>
> = 44.1 x 16 x 5 / 8 kB
>
> = 441 kB

Q18 Calculate the file size in bytes of a radio jingle lasting 15 seconds, using a sample rate of 8,000Hz and a 16 bit sample resolution.

8.6 – Compression

When data is transmitted across the Internet it will go through many different physical links between routers. The connection from a computer or a LAN into the Internet is likely to be the slowest part of this route, as you probably know from experience. At home you may have quite a slow network connection and it may take a while for web pages to load.

One way of speeding up the rate at which files can be transmitted across the Internet is to compress them to make them smaller. Smaller files take less time to transmit over a network.

Understanding how compression affects files is important as the type of compression selected will affect how the image looks or the audio track sounds. The final use of the file will dictate how much you can compress it and still have a file that is useable.

To summarise, compression is used in order to:

- reduce the amount of storage needed on a computer to save files
- allow large files to be transmitted as an email attachment; many email servers limit the size of a file that can be sent and compression can reduce the file size allow to allow users to send the file
- allow a file to be transmitted in less time, owing to the smaller file size

Lossy compression

Lossy compression is a data encoding method where files are compressed by removing some of the detail. For example, photographs can be stored using fewer colours so fewer bits are needed per pixel. This type of compression is used to compress images, audio files and video files, where it is easy to recognise an image or sound clip even if some data is missing.

A bitmap image (.bmp) or .png file is a lossless version of an image. If you save the same photograph as a JPEG file then it is still a high quality image with a colour depth of 24 bits but some of the data is lost where it is unlikely to be noticed.

If you save the same picture as a GIF file, then you make the file size much smaller as you only use 8 bits instead of 24 bits per pixel. The human eye can tell the difference at this stage. You will see solid blocks of colour instead of gradual transitions in the photograph. However, for small pictures on websites that will only be viewed as a thumbnail, GIF files are fine and take less time to load on a webpage.

Here is a section of a photograph blown up so you can see the difference:

JPEG version

GIF version

Lossy compression formats are show below:

Type	File suffix	Compression Type	Explanation
Bitmap	.bmp	-	Uncompressed still image file
JPEG	.jpg	Lossy	Good for photographs. Colour depth = 24 bits, RGB, 16.7 million different colours
Windows Media Player	.wmv .wav	Lossy	Audio files: Files are not as small as MP3
MP3	.mp3	Lossy	Audio files: Designed for downloading music from the Internet. In MP3 format you could fit 120 songs on a CD.
MPEG -1	.mpg	Lossy	Video files: Suitable for small low-resolution sequences on CD
MPEG-2	.mp2	Lossy	Video files: Suitable for full-screen, high resolution video on DVD

Lossless compression

This is a data encoding method where files are compressed but no data is lost – an essential factor for text and data files. For example, bank records must keep all of the data; you cannot transmit a bank statement and miss out a few zeros because they don't matter too much!

It could be used to compress data files, for example by 'zipping' them using a utility program such as WinZip, before attaching them to an email.

The following table shows different file types and file extensions used for lossless compression formats:

Type	File suffix	Compression Type	Explanation
Portable Network Graphic	.png	Lossless	Colour depth = 24 bits, RGB, 16.7 million different colours
Graphic Interchange Format	.gif	Lossless	Colour depth = 8 bits (only 256 colours) Good for images with large areas of solid colour Ideal for web graphics Although this is a lossless compression, images with higher colour depths are often converted into GIFs to make them smaller (This process is called 'quantisation' but is not in the GCSE specification.)
QuickTime	.mov	Lossless	Audio files
Portable Document Format	.pdf	-	A (usually uncompressed) document format that is universally accessible.

Exercises

1. (a) Add the following two 8-bit binary numbers. [2]

    1 0 0 1 1 0 1 1
    0 1 0 1 0 1 0 0

    (b) An overflow error can occur when adding two 8-bit binary numbers.
    Describe what is meant by an overflow error. [2]

    OCR A451 June 2014 Qu 3

2. The number 73 could be a denary number or a hex number.

    (a) If 73 is a hex number, calculate its value as a denary number.

    You **must** show your working. [2]

    (b) If 73 is a denary number, calculate its value as a hex number.

    You **must** show your working. [2]

3. Numbers can be represented in denary, binary or hexadecimal.

(a) (i) Convert the binary number 01101001 to denary, showing your working. [2]

(ii) Convert the number 154 to binary. [2]

(b) The security code for an alarm system is a long binary number which begins

10001111100101111011 …

The technicians prefer to use hexadecimal to enter the security code.

(i) When the number is converted into hexadecimal, the first two digits are 8F as shown below.

Complete the gaps to show the next three digits.

Binary	1000	1111	1001	0111	1011
Hexadecimal	8	F	……..	……..	……….

[3]

(ii) Explain why the technicians prefer to use hexadecimal. [2]

OCR A451 June 2013 Qu 5

4. (a) Explain why data is stored in computers in a binary format. [2]

(b) In the ASCII character set, the character codes for the first three capital letters are given below.

Letter	ASCII character code
A	0100 0001
B	0100 0010
C	0100 0011

(i) State how the ASCII character set is used to represent text in a computer. [2]

(ii) Convert the word CAB into binary using the ASCII character set. [2]

(iii) Explain why the ASCII character set is **not** suitable for representing text in all the languages of the world. [2]

OCR A451 Jan 2013 Qu 8

5. When recording a sound file on a computer, the sound needs to be sampled.

(i) Describe how sampling is used when storing sound. [2]

(ii) Explain the effect of the sampling interval on the size and quality of the sound file recorded. [3]

OCR A451 Jan 2013 Qu 6

6. Files are often compressed before they are sent over the internet.

(a) State what is meant by compression. [1]

State **one** advantage of compressing files before sending them over the internet. [1]

(b) Two types of compression are lossy and lossless.

State which type of compression is most appropriate for each of the following and explain why it is appropriate.

(i) Downloading the source code of a large program. [3]

(ii) Streaming a large video file. [3]

OCR A451/01 June 2013 Qu 8

Index

OCR GCSE J276 (9-1) Specification map

Computer systems

		Section 1	Section 2	Section 3	Section 4	Section 5	Section 6	Section 7	Section 8
1.1	Systems architecture	✓							
1.2	Memory	✓							
1.3	Storage	✓							
1.4	Wired and wireless networks		✓						
1.5	Network topologies, protocols and layers		✓						
1.6	System security			✓					
1.7	System software			✓					
1.8	Ethical, legal and cultural concerns				✓				

Computational thinking, algorithms and programming

		Section 1	Section 2	Section 3	Section 4	Section 5	Section 6	Section 7	Section 8
2.1	Algorithms					✓			
2.2	Programming techniques						✓		
2.3	Producing robust programs							✓	
2.4	Computational logic						✓		
2.5	Translators and facilities of languages							✓	
2.6	Data representation								✓

The content in each section of the textbook covers the same specification points as the corresponding downloadable teaching unit, e.g. Section 1 complements Unit 1.